T0203181

Sounding Heaven and Earth

Sounding Heaven and Earth

A Poet's Corner Collection

Malcolm Guite

CANTERBURY
PRESS
Norwich

© Malcolm Guite 2023

First published in 2023 by the Canterbury Press Norwich
Editorial office
3rd Floor, Invicta House
108–114 Golden Lane
London EC1Y 0TG, UK

www.canterburypress.co.uk

Canterbury Press is an imprint of Hymns Ancient & Modern Ltd
(a registered charity)

Hymns Ancient & Modern® is a registered trademark of
Hymns Ancient & Modern Ltd
13A Hellesdon Park Road, Norwich,
Norfolk NR6 5DR, UK

Malcolm Guite's poem 'Our Burning World' is used by permission
of Stainer & Bell Ltd, 23 Gruneisen Road, London N3 1LS,
www.stainer.co.uk. All rights reserved.

British Library Cataloguing in Publication data

A catalogue record for this book is available
from the British Library

ISBN 978-1-78622-539-9

Typeset by Regent Typesetting
Printed and bound in Great Britain by
CPI Group (UK) Ltd

Contents

Foreword   xi

 1 Little Steps   1
 2 Born of Water   3
 3 Multum in Parvo   5
 4 A Poet for January   7
 5 A Coral Rose   10
 6 Mummers at Midnight   12
 7 Home at Last   14
 8 A Blessing on Ronald Blythe   16
 9 Weather Words   18
10 Candlemas   20
11 Reading Milton   22
12 Love and the Martyr   24
13 Thank You for Waiting   26
14 Above and Beneath the Floorboards   28
15 Nashotah House   30
16 Remembering the Ash   32
17 Launch Out into the Deep   34
18 That Morning   36
19 Norfolk Pamments   38
20 Remembering Yeats in a Time of War   40
21 Merlin's Barrow   43
22 On the Thames   45
23 A Golden Era   48

24	Cherry Blossoms	50
25	Advice	52
26	A Minor Exorcism	54
27	A Breath of Heaven	56
28	At a Consecration	58
29	Musing on Psalm 84	60
30	In King's College Chapel	62
31	In Brontë Country	64
32	A Prayer Under the New Moon	66
33	Stevenson's Pipe	68
34	Ranworth Rose	70
35	Distant Jubilation	72
36	Waiting for the Tide	74
37	Trinity Sunday	76
38	A Little Reminder of Liberty	78
39	The Ancient Mariner	80
40	Mysterious Ascensions	82
41	The Right Word	84
42	Pentecost and Translation	86
43	The Kingfisher and the Heron	88
44	Returning to Ely	90
45	Remembering Shelley	92
46	A Choice of Signs	94
47	Hide and Seek	96
48	Poetry as a Way of Knowing	98
49	A Wake-Up Call	100
50	From a Celtic Roundhouse	102
51	Do Different	105
52	In Southwell Minster	107

53	Under the Mercy	109
54	Remembering Larkin	111
55	Moonlight and Sacrament	113
56	Seven Sunken Englands	115
57	Holding and Letting Go	118
58	A Coronation Psalm	120
59	At the Treacle Well	122
60	A Fish Out of Water?	124
61	On Lindisfarne	126
62	The Fascination with What's Difficult	128
63	A Few Gleanings	131
64	A Door In and Out	133
65	An Unveiling	135
66	With Alfred at Wantage	137
67	Steeped in Ireland	139
68	The Wind in the Trees	141
69	Rereading 'Eden Rock'	143
70	In the Woods	145
71	A Debt to David Scott	148
72	A Winter's Ale	150
73	A Scion of the Sheltering Tree	152
74	Rereading Keats	154
75	Christmas Lights	156
76	Ear Worms	158
	Acknowledgements and References	161

In memory of Ronald Blythe 1922–2023

Foreword

The title of this new collection of my little pieces for the *Church Times* is drawn, as were the titles of the two previous collections, from the poetry of George Herbert.

To be 'sounding heaven and earth' would be a large claim for any writer to make, and while Herbert's poetry, and particularly the poem 'Prayer', from which this phrase is drawn, does indeed sound heaven and earth, and explore and open up for us the heights and depths of our spiritual life, I would hesitate to make such a claim for this collection of momentary pauses and reflections, though they may sometimes offer a glimpse of 'Heaven in ordinary'.

In what sense, then, might these brief essays be called 'soundings'? The full line from which my title comes is: 'The Christian plummet, sounding heaven and earth', one of the 26 emblems of prayer Herbert offers in his densely packed sonnet. I love the tentative and exploratory nature of Herbert's image. This is not the language of blazing certainty, and certainly not the language of arrogant assertion. Herbert's image summons up the linesman with his 'plummet', his lead weight at the end of a knotted cord. He stands at the bow as his ship creeps forward, perhaps through fog or darkness, into uncharted waters, and lowers the plummet into the water, feeling the knots, each tied at a fathom's length, as they run through his fingers, waiting for the weight to touch bottom. Then he calls back to the helmsman: 'Full fathom five, by the mark! Yes, we have enough depth beneath our keel, it's safe to go forward, we're not yet in danger of running aground.' It's a fine image for prayer, for that time spent with God when, however dark or confused things seem, we get a feel for the depth beneath our keel, a feel for the depth of the soul, and the greater depth of Christ's love, an assurance that God is not just in the unattainable heavens above but down here with us, down here even below us, that 'underneath are the everlasting arms'.

I don't pretend to such depth in all these pieces, but writing them was for me a way of taking soundings, pausing for a moment in the bustle of life to savour an experience, to hold it for a moment to the light before it slips away and say: 'What does this mean? What does it suggest? Has it anything to teach me? Are there perhaps some hidden depths here?'

A glimpse of wild swimmers suddenly takes me back to the waters of baptism, rereading a poem of Yeats at the start of the Ukraine war gives me the grip and the language to pray into that tragedy, a chance encounter with a cat in an Oxford graveyard brings me to the grave and to the revolutionary and ever-more relevant thought of Charles Williams, 'the oddest' of the Oxford Inklings.

Sometimes the soundings in these pages take another sense of that word: a delight in sound itself, in the sounds of certain words, in the music of bells, in the way the music of Scotland and Ireland has been re-born and revoiced in America. There are reflections too on reading, on the sheer pleasure of books and the conversations they strike up with one another in one's mind, as one stills one's own voice and listens to the authors talking across the ages, sounding one another out.

The reader may also notice, as they journey through the book, that, like my first volume of poetry, they are also 'sounding the seasons'. For these little essays touch on Christmas and Candlemas, on the ardours of Lent and the joys of Easter, and on the passing of the seasons of the earth, on the pleasures, the perils and the warnings of our weather.

They will also sometimes hear other sounds too, the

sounds that mark the arrivals and departures of our fellow pilgrims, they will hear the bells of jubilation for our late Queen's Diamond Jubilee, and also her passing bell. And softer, not so much in the public eye or ear, the passing bell of my great predecessor Ronald Blythe, and I am glad to include in this collection a piece I wrote when I heard the news that he had left us: 'A Blessing on Ronald Blythe'. You would not have this volume in your hands had he not created the space and the precedent when he sounded out his *Word from Wormingford*, and I dedicate this Poet's Corner collection to his memory.

1

Little Steps

As we all take our first, possibly faltering, steps into the new year, I have found myself not only taking, but also constructing, some new steps. My Christmas present from Maggie was a lovely set of wooden folding library steps – essential, as the bookshelves in my smaller retirement study now go up to the ceiling.

But there was one small catch: my present came in the form of a flatpack, and was not so much a set of folding steps as an assortment of bits of wood, screws, bolts, Allen keys, and, on a single sheet, a densely printed, and scarcely comprehensible, set of 'instructions'. In fact, they were not instructions: just a parts list, and two inscrutable diagrams.

As I spread the pieces out on the living-room carpet, I was reminded of the anecdote in *Zen and the Art of Motorcycle Maintenance*, in which the author is asked to assemble a Japanese rotisserie and finds that the first 'step' in the poorly translated assembly instructions reads: 'Before Assembling Rotisserie, First Attain Peace of Mind.'

This phrase has become a mantra in our household, recited before we undertake anything daunting. I had not the time, before assembling the steps, to undergo Zazen training, or to listen earnestly for the sound of one hand clapping; but I did have my daughter at hand to help me with our 3D jigsaw puzzle, to help me guess how dowel A might be offered up to slat J, and generally to keep me calm.

Between us, we somehow succeeded in transforming the scattered bits and pieces into a beautiful, serviceable little piece of furniture in dark grained wood, which looks far better in my study, and is far safer, than the various wobbly chairs and boxes of unfiled papers on which I had once

1

been precariously balancing when I reached for the higher shelves. Now, I can mount serenely and explore those upper shelves with ease.

Most of the assembly was done while kneeling on the floor. I had, as it were, to diminish myself and lower my gaze in order, finally, to straighten up, to rise, to be lifted to a new perspective on my study and my books. Surveying my shelves and study from the top of the new steps, I feel as though I have enacted a parable, or actualised a ritual pattern; for that lowering of the gaze before it is raised, that assiduous and concentrated effort with little bits and pieces, which itself somehow enables a new way to rise and a new perspective, is just as true of poetry and of prayer as it was of my step-assembly.

As Seamus Heaney testified in *Crediting Poetry*, there had to be years 'bowed to the desk like some monk bowed over his prie-dieu, some dutiful contemplative pivoting his understanding' before he could finally and happily 'straighten up' and 'make space in [his] reckoning and imagination for the marvellous'.

Years of practice at bringing the parts of a poem together was, it turns out, good preparation for my furniture assembly; for my hope is that my poems, too, once assembled, might offer little steps: a platform raised, however slightly, to give the reader new access and new perspective. And, as for prayer, that kneeling to be raised, that closing of the eyes to see – well, it turns out that my completed library steps also form their own kind of kneeler: a poet's prie-dieu.

2

Born of Water

I have a great admiration for 'wild swimmers': those courageous souls who fling themselves into rivers and lakes, and reclaim – indeed, proclaim – for all of us, our natural affinity for these waters and our right to revel in them. I swam a little in the Cam myself in my Cambridge days, and earlier still in the lakes and rivers of Ontario, as a teenager in Canada; but these days, I must confess, I would rather be coddled in the warmer waters of our local spa.

Nevertheless, I am always impressed by the pictures and video clips that we are shown every January of intrepid swimmers out on New Year's Day, sometimes breaking the ice to plunge into the freezing waters of lochs and lakes and tarns. Even on the screen, even from the warmth of your couch, you can almost feel the courage, the excitement, the exhilaration of the leap, the plunge, the immersion, and then the emergence of spluttering, happy, slightly shocked, and yet radiant, faces in this annual ritual.

I have heard some of these folk talk about this experience in ecstatic, sometimes spiritual or religious, language. And, in a way, they are right. It is surely an echo, a kind of mimesis, a parallel enactment of the great immersion and recovery, the plunging and renewal of baptism. 'I come up fresh and tingling,' they say, 'refreshed, renewed, reborn into the new year.'

Baptism is, after all, the great ritual of death and rebirth, in which we are plunged with Christ into 'the deep waters of death' to emerge 'born again of water and the Spirit'. Indeed, the size and shape of our old church fonts makes it clear that infants were once immersed in them rather than politely affused, and the birth imagery of the baby drawn dripping

3

from the waters and placed in her mother's arms must have been unmistakable. This was why Lancelot Andrewes, in one of his many pithy apothegms, said: 'The font is the womb of the church.'

There is a beautiful fourteenth-century font in St Edward King and Martyr, in Cambridge, whose great stone bowl appears to be supported effortlessly, almost to float, on the wings of the angels carved beneath it. I loved conducting baptisms there, and out of that experience came a sonnet in which I drew on Andrewes's insight, as well as recalling Hildegard of Bingen's beautiful saying that she was 'a feather on the breath of God'. It's good to recall it now, as every baptism is renewed in the renewal of the year:

Baptism

Love's hidden thread has drawn us to the font,
A wide womb floating on the breath of God,
Feathered with seraph wings, lit with the swift
Lightning of praise, with thunder over-spread,
And under-girded with an unheard song,
Calling through water, fire, darkness, pain,
Calling us to the life for which we long,
Yearning to bring us to our birth again.
Again the breath of God is on the waters
In whose reflecting face our candles shine,
Again he draws from death the sons and daughters
For whom he bid the elements combine.
As living stones around a font today,
Rejoice with those who roll the stone away.

3

Multum in Parvo

Where do poems live? As a pattern of print on a page, or only as a song in the air?

There is one sense in which poems don't live on the page at all, but, rather, slumber there, waiting for the reader to breathe them into being. The flat white paper and the little black letters in their serried rows are no more than a form of transport, a convenient means of delivery. Living and capacious meanings, gentle allusions, compressed images, and numinous and musical phrases are all jostled together like passengers on a train, constrained for a while, but only constrained in order to be released – to expand, to step out, and to explore with the reader the opening landscapes of their heart and soul; for the reader's heart is the true destination of every poem.

And, in that sense, it doesn't matter what edition you read them in. It is true that a sumptuous edition of Keats with thick creamy pages, beautiful black-letter printing, and a fine leather binding does seem a fitting vehicle to carry such rich freight, but 'Ode to a Nightingale' would still work its magic: the nightingale would sing for you, and the magic casements would still open on perilous seas in fairy lands forlorn, even if you read the poem in some tatty old school edition, torn and smeared with inky thumbprints and defaced with pointless annotations. I have been happy to find that poem and bid it rise from the page in both kinds of book.

But, sometimes, the presentation of a poem is so apt, so thoughtful, or so surprising that it does, indeed, enhance our understanding and experience of the poem itself. Or so I felt when I was presented with what appeared to be no more than a little matchbox. It was beautiful, to be sure: the outer box had the lovely image of a finely drawn blackbird on a green background, on which were also drawn, as though miniatures from a botanical handbook, willows, willowherb, and grass; and, on the other side of the box, against the same meadow-green, were meadowsweet and many of the grasses and flowers that one might find in an English meadow.

But, when I slid the box open, I found, not matches, but a long thin strip of paper folded, in a concertina, to nestle in the matchbox, and, on the topmost side, facing me as I opened the box, the words '"Adlestrop", Edward Thomas'. Lifting that leaf delicately out and letting the whole unfold and expand, I found on one side just the word Adlestrop, printed across the fold lines in the lettering of the old railway-station signs against the same green background, again with the blackbird, the willowherb and meadowsweet, and, delicately drawn, a steam engine; then, on the other side, the poem itself.

One had to draw out and unfold the little concertina to read it, but there it all was, from its opening affirmation 'Yes. I remember Adlestrop' to its evocation of that June afternoon at the lonely station, the hissing of steam, the silence, the glimpses of the meadows and the meadowsweet, the unexpected song of the blackbird, and, at last, its evocation

... mistier,
Farther and farther, all the birds
Of Oxfordshire and Gloucestershire.

The exquisite little edition that I held in my hand was itself a perfect emblem of the poem that it contained: something small and delicately formed, which, once opened, could expand and unfold till it opened and evoked the heart of England.

4

A Poet for January

Recently, I found myself walking rather grimly through the streets of Norwich in a bleak, sleety January drizzle. My hands deep in the pockets of my old tweed greatcoat, which was already becoming damp and heavy, I asked myself the obvious question: Where is the poetry of drizzle?

There's plenty celebrating winds and wild weather: Shelley's glorious 'Ode to the West Wind', for example, and plenty that speaks of that mirroring of weather and mood which we so often experience, as in Keats's lovely verse in his 'Ode On Melancholy':

> But when the melancholy fit shall fall
> Sudden from heaven like a weeping cloud,
> That fosters the droop-headed flowers all,
> And hides the green hill in an April shroud.

But what about this dreich and melancholy drizzle augmenting our January blues? Almost as I asked the question, the answer came in a couple of lines of Tennyson's, which almost perfectly described my experience at that moment:

> And ghastly thro' the drizzling rain
> On the bald street breaks the blank day.

Reciting these lines doesn't change the weather, but there is a certain grim satisfaction in knowing that one's own experience of it has been so perfectly expressed.

T. S. Eliot reckoned that Tennyson had the finest ear for the sound of the English language of any poet, and, unsurprisingly, the author of *The Waste Land* singled out these two lines for particular praise, especially for the sheer downbeat plodding sound of the eight one-syllable words that make up the tetrameter of that final line.

It is, in fact, the final line of the shortest and, in many ways, most moving of the poems that make up Tennyson's sequence *In Memoriam*, a sequence that usually has its national moment on New Year's Eve or 1 January, when the ringing of our church bells is often accompanied with a reading of the great moment of recovery later in the sequence:

> Ring out, wild bells, to the wild sky,
> The flying cloud, the frosty light:
> The year is dying in the night;
> Ring out, wild bells, and let him die.

But Tennyson is not just for Christmas and New Year, and I'm glad to have him as a companion for those bleaker days later in January and February when we feel we simply have to hunker down and get through it. *In Memoriam* deals both truthfully and beautifully with depression and darkness, and especially, as its title suggests, with bereavement.

The short poem whose last lines I was remembering in the Norfolk drizzle begins with Tennyson, whether waking or in dreams is not clear, visiting the house of his friend Hallam, only to realise, once more, that he is gone for ever: a jolting experience of repeated reminders of absence, which any bereaved person will recognise. The poem doesn't remove or even heal the grief, but I, for one, find comfort and a kind of solace in knowing that my own griefs have been experienced and so well expressed by others:

Dark house, by which once more I stand
Here in the long unlovely street,
Doors, where my heart was used to beat
So quickly, waiting for a hand,
A hand that can be clasp'd no more.

The time comes, of course, when Tennyson can 'Ring out, ring out my mournful rhymes But ring the fuller minstrel in'; but I am glad that he was so honest with us about the time that it took to get there.

5

A Coral Rose

It was a relief, listening, the other morning, to the *Today* programme, to be taken for a while out of the shallow and murky waters of British politics and into the pristine depths of the Pacific, and to hear that, off the coast of Tahiti, divers have discovered, at unusual depth, a perfectly formed reef of rose-shaped corals.

'It was magical to witness giant, beautiful rose corals, which stretch for as far as the eye can see. It was like a work of art,' said the French photographer Alexis Rosenfeld, who led the team of international divers who made the discovery.

I've always loved coral. From my childhood memories of Ballantyne's *The Coral Island* (the innocent progenitor of Golding's darker book) to the beautiful pictures of angel fish flitting among the reefs in *Something Rich and Strange*, Robert E. Schroeder's book on night diving, which inspired my teenage years and made me want to be a marine biologist, there was a coral strand running through my imagination. When I turned from biology to the less demanding vocation of poetry, there was still a magical aura about the word 'coral', there in the passage of *The Tempest* to which Schroeder's title alludes:

> Full fathom five thy father lies;
> Of his bones are coral made;
> Those are pearls that were his eyes:
> Nothing of him that doth fade,
> But doth suffer a sea-change
> Into something rich and strange.

Shakespeare suggests, hauntingly, that, amid the corals and the pearls, there is some rich transformation, even in death, of our own humanity: a foretaste of resurrection. And that, of course, is the theme of the play; for, as in a baptism, that mimesis of death and resurrection, all who seemed drowned in the tempest are miraculously drawn from the waters and restored to life again.

So, to hear on the radio the description of these magical rose corals already summoned many echoes and images in my head. These distant rose shapes in the deep evoked for me Yeats's early invocation:

Far-off, most secret, and inviolate Rose,
Enfold me in my hour of hours; where those
Who sought thee in the Holy Sepulchre,
Or in the wine-vat, dwell beyond the stir
And tumult of defeated dreams; and deep ...

And so we find another rose in the deep.

Later, I looked up the story online, and saw a wonderful film of little fish flitting in and out of the 'petals' as divers glided above the vast and yet delicate multifoliate roses of coral, rose-shaped and rose-red in the diver's lights. It was marvellous and actual – and all of it unbleached, uncorroded, as yet untouched by climate change; for the reef lies deep enough to be protected from the bleaching effects of the warming ocean.

A rose by any other name would smell as sweet, but there is something wonderful about how another life, the living, growing creature that is the coral, can take on that same shape and suggest to us, even in the cold depths, the gentle exhalations of a summer's day.

6

Mummers at Midnight

We were treated to a Christmastide tradition in our local, the White Swan, when a troupe, or 'side', of mummers came in, as promised, to enact their play. They came somewhat past their hour, but this was understandable, as they had been mumming earlier, at the Hop Inn, where, it seems, they hopped and danced and played so well that the locals detained them for a few more drinks.

But, once they assembled at the White Swan, we were well rewarded for our patience; for they played with great gusto, and with a wonderful and easygoing mixture of the old and the new. All the old characters were there: St George; the Turkish Knight; Father Christmas (properly decked in green fir-trimmed robe and crowned with holly – none of this post-Coca-Cola red and white); Beelzebub, duly horned; and, of course, the Doctor, with his magical life-restoring serum.

There was also an extra that I'd not seen in mumming before: Beelzebub was accompanied by his monstrous hell-hound Black Shuck, who did much more of the scarifying than his master. This was fitting for East Anglia; for it is in this part of England that tales of the dog abound. There is, for example, an account of him running through a church in Bungay, on the southern edge of the Broads, in *A Straunge and Terrible Wunder* by Abraham Fleming, in 1577: 'This black dog, or the divel in such a likenesse (God hee knoweth al who worketh all,) running all along down the body of the church with great swiftnesse, and incredible haste, among the people, in a visible form and shape …'

The Edwardian folklorist W. A. Dutt went so far as to suggest that these tales of Black Shuck represent a folk memory from the days when the Vikings settled in these parts: a memory of 'the old Scandinavian myth of the black hound of Odin, brought to us by the Vikings who long ago settled down on the Norfolk coast'.

But this mummers' play, for all its old traditions enshrining folk memory, both pagan and Christian, was also played for laughs, with plenty of contemporary references, from the pantomime punning – when, having been told in rhyming couplets that the Turkish knight had been 'slayed', the whole company, and, indeed, the whole pub, burst into the Slade anthem 'Merry Xmas Everybody' – to more serious echoes: when the Doctor arrived and revived the afflicted to great rejoicing, there was more than a nod to the heroic NHS during Covid. We all applauded the resurrection of the dead.

I was glad to see it all still going on, notwithstanding the efforts of the Puritans, also numerous in these parts, to ban it altogether. For them, 'mummery' was a term of abuse, and, indeed, they went so far as to call the eucharist a 'popish mummery'. They were wrong, of course, to the extent that they meant that word to signify a foolish play of falsehood; but, if we were to take mumming in its deepest sense, as a dramatic representation – indeed, recreation in the present – of a collective memory of the death and resurrection that changed everything, then maybe to call the sacrament a 'mummery' is to hint at another facet of its mystery.

The White Swan stands hard by St Nicholas's, our parish church, and, just as the landlady of the White Swan welcomed the mummers, so I was glad to see that she herself and some of the mummers were welcomed and exchanged the Peace with us all at the midnight mass.

7

Home at Last

I'm home at last, in the familiar and comfortable armchair of my little study, after another week of intensive and exhausting lecturing in the States – and what a pleasure it is to be back!

There is, of course, as much to admire as to deplore in America, as in most countries; but there is also, as they rightly say, no place like home. I always enjoy the work itself, and the people I meet, but one disadvantage of frequent travel in our age is that you usually stay in identikit soulless hotel chains, whose lobbies, lifts, corridors and rooms all look the same, and offer no sign of place or character.

They could be anywhere. They have the same grey carpets, faux modern art, huge television screens, which I never watch, constantly whirring central heating, a myriad of little lights on everything from coffee-makers, screens and fire alarms to bedside digital clocks, none of which you can turn off, and which wink at you balefully all night unless you contrive to cover them with your discarded clothes; and, worst of all, those dirty grey windows that you cannot open, though you are desperate for a breath of fresh air and a sense of where you actually are.

Only so much of that alienating placelessness can I take; so, I sometimes sit in my hotel room and imagine my own study, mentally shelving the walls and filling them with books, all old favourites, cluttering the icily empty desk, if there is one, with piles of imaginary books and papers, leather-bound journals with half-written poems, pens, ink bottles, and, of course, pipes: some in their racks, some resting on their bowls in ashtrays, and some half-smoked, leaning precariously on the book piles where I left them.

If I try hard, I can even imagine the aroma of my study, the subtle combination of old tomes and aromatic tobacco. I am comforted for a second or two, but then it's gone, and I am back in the alienating bleak minimalism that some design committee decided would please, or at least not offend, the average customer.

I sometimes wish that I had been a writer in an earlier age. The familiar essays by the likes of Hilaire Belloc and G. K. Chesterton often describe their travels, and they always seem to stay in glorious old coaching inns, each with its distinctive atmosphere, its local ales and its magnificently Dickensian characters. They give you the savour and flavour of each little town or village, and you rejoice with them in the sheer variety and diversity with which the map of England is speckled and chequered.

Now, Chesterton was a man of such wit and good humour that he could probably have found something beneficent and thankful to say about even the blandest of my hotel rooms; for, after all, it was he who said that 'an inconvenience is simply an adventure wrongly considered'; but I have not yet attained to his breadth, his unfailing enthusiasm, or his saintly optimism, and my efforts flag after a day or two.

At least it means, though, that when I am back in this armchair among the friendly and familiar scatter of books and pipes, I am as genuinely delighted and as profoundly thankful as Chesterton himself.

8

A Blessing on Ronald Blythe

Like so many readers of this paper, and many more beyond, I was sorry to hear of the death of Ronald Blythe, and, at the same time, stirred afresh to gratitude for his life and work. I always enjoyed his 'Word from Wormingford': his close observation of nature, his eye for significant detail, his sense of the presence of the past, and the almost personal presence of his great literary predecessors: John Clare, Thomas Traherne, George Herbert, Nicholas Ferrar.

Herbert and Ferrar were especially akin to him, for they both gave their best in their living and their writing to tiny country parishes far from the spotlight and attention of the world, but always close to the Kingdom; and so, too, did Blythe.

Although I felt I knew him well from the close companionship of his writing, I met him only once in person, but it was a signal and memorable occasion. We were once asked jointly to lead the annual pilgrimage to Little Gidding, walking from Leighton Bromswold, the church which Herbert restored, five miles to Little Gidding, where Herbert's friend Nicholas Ferrar had formed a community, where the manuscript of *The Temple* was sent after Herbert's death, and, of course, the place that inspired the last of the *Four Quartets*.

I was to preach at Leighton, and Blythe was to preach at Little Gidding.

I was very much in awe of him, and glad that I was preaching first and didn't have to follow him; but I was delighted to meet him. He was charming, personable, a little shy, I think, and certainly carried no stand-offishness or sense of his literary status. As we walked and talked together, on a dismally wet day, I sensed that he was walking in the company of invisible as well as visible pilgrims. He mentioned some of our contemporaries, and then, in the same breath, would quote Clare or Herbert, Herrick or Hopkins, with such natural familiarity that I would not have been surprised to turn around and find them walking at our side, or just ahead of us.

We arrived, drenched, at the Giddings – indeed, such were our numbers that he spoke at Steeple Gidding, as we would not all have fitted in the little chapel which was the end of our pilgrimage. He spoke about the Ferrars, about their commitment to place and people, their refusal of the glamour and glitter of court and city, of what it meant for them to be, in their phrase, 'in the right good old way,' and of what that might mean for us.

I think of him now, walking ahead of us in that good old way towards heaven's gate, and bless him in words I wrote once at Little Gidding, for Nicholas Ferrar:

From the folds of sleep, the late
Risers wake to find you gone, and pray
Through pain and grief to bless your journey home;
Those last glad steps in the right good old way
Up to the door where Love will bid you welcome.
Love draws us too, towards your grave and haven
We greet you at the very gate of Heaven.

9

Weather Words

For my annual January dip into the poetry of Robert Burns, I found myself reading his celebrated poem 'To a Mouse' aloud, and thus really tasting the words, savouring the sounds, getting the full pungency of his Scots dialect. I can't recite it as well as my mother, a true Scotswoman, used to do each year, but I give it a try in her memory.

What struck me this time round was the vivid accuracy of the descriptions of bleak winter weather in words that sound like, and almost embody, the severity that they denote: 'An' bleak December's win's ensuing, Baith snell an' keen!'

'Snell' is such a telling word – I can feel the wind whistling through me as I say it. It carries so much meaning that the *Dictionaries of the Scots Language* use five separate English words just to give a sense of it: 'biting, keen, piercing, bitter, severe'.

And then, a little later in the poem, as Burns thinks of the poor mouse turned out to face the elements like some evicted crofter, he says:

Now thou's turned out, for a' thy trouble,
But house or hald,
To thole the Winter's sleety dribble,
An' cranreuch cauld!

There's such rich language in that verse: 'Thole' carries much more of grim determination than its Latinate English equivalent, 'endure'. 'Sleety dribble' is a phrase that we have retained in English for the very good reason that we often need it, but we have no exact equivalent of 'cranreuch'. Here, the Scots has retained an originally Gaelic term, *crann reodhach*, 'frosty tree': a poetic suggestion of the branching crystals of hoar frost, although *cran* also means to shrink or shrivel, which adds to the sense of the bleak and cold, picked up by Burns in following 'cranreuch' with 'cauld'. But it's the sound of the word 'cranreuch' which carries so much more of the experience of the crinkling crunching of frost beneath one's feet than our term, hoar frost.

English poets, though, are also more than capable of giving us the bleak winter soundscape, as well as the outer descriptions of its weather. In *Sir Gawain and the Green Knight* (the fine Middle English poem, not the execrable film), there's a wonderful description of the weather as Gawain journeys north to meet his fate and keep his tryst with the Green Knight, when the poet says that the weather was a far worse enemy than any warfare:

> For werre wrathed hym not so much þat wynter nas wors,
> When þe colde cler water fro þe cloudez schadde,
> And fres er hit falle myȝt to þe fale erþe;
> Ner slayn wyth þe slete he sleped in his yrnes.

Jessie Weston renders this in modern English as: 'Yet he cared not so much for the strife, what he deemed worse was when the cold clear water was shed from the clouds and froze ere it fell on the fallow ground. More nights than enough he slept in his harness on the bare rocks, near slain with the sleet.' This keeps some of the memorable phrases, such as 'slain with the sleet', but misses the simple concentrated alliterative pungency of 'winter was worse'.

As I step out into a dreich January day, its winds flinging freezing sleet into my face, I'm glad to have such a word-hoard to call upon, to know that I am not the only poet to have trudged through the 'cranreuch cauld' or to feel that he is being 'slayn with the slete'.

10

Candlemas

Candlemas is one of my favourite feasts for two reasons. First, it brings the arc of the Christmas story to a beautiful conclusion, carrying it to the brink of Lent. Second, it brings together, in the same scene, and at the same pivotal moment, the oldest and the youngest people in the story. Indeed, if we think of Christ in his infancy, Mary and Joseph in their prime, and Simeon and Anna in extreme old age, and then unite all the ages and stages of human life, this scene in the Temple has some claim to be the first all-age service.

When Eamon Duffy's monumental *The Stripping of the Altars* first appeared, I was very moved by the chapter that he devoted to Candlemas, as a worked example of how the service, and the gospel at its heart, was owned and entered into by both community and church. All the candles that would be used in the parish that year – both in the church and to light people's homes – were brought into the church and blessed: all these little outer lights brought to the true Light that lightens the world, to be kindled in spirit, to be 'dipped and glamoured' (to borrow a phrase of Heaney's), immersed in the aura of the sacrament. I loved, too, Duffy's account of community participation: the different guilds bringing their votive candles, the oldest inhabitants of the parish joining the procession as Simeon and Anna.

But, if Candlemas was so consonant with community life then, it is positively and prophetically counter-cultural now. We live in a culture that ruthlessly divides and separates the ages and stages of life: the aged are siphoned off into retirement complexes and care homes; couples starting out together, and those with young families, can scarcely afford anywhere to live; and, when they can, it's nowhere near their parents and grandparents.

Even in church, the one place where we might reconstitute a more balanced community, we often find a sort of liturgical apartheid. Children are taken off to separate rooms; the elderly, put off by razzmatazz and innovation, congregate to the eight o'clock Prayer Book service; and those who are left muddle through with something in the middle. But, perhaps at Candlemas, at least, we can all be together.

When I came to write my 'Candlemas' sonnet for *Sounding the Seasons*, I rejoiced that Simeon and Anna, economically unproductive as they might be, still had a place in the Temple. But I also reflected on how, even then, Mary and Joseph had to overcome some barriers to get in – barriers which their son would one day throw down:

Candlemas

They came, as called, according to the Law.
Though they were poor and had to keep things simple,
They moved in grace, in quietness, in awe,
For God was coming with them to His temple.
Amidst the outer court's commercial bustle
They'd waited hours, enduring shouts and shoves,
Buyers and sellers, sensing one more hustle,
Had made a killing on the two young doves.
They come at last with us to Candlemas
And keep the day the prophecies came true;
We share with them, amidst our busyness,
The peace that Simeon and Anna knew.
For Candlemas still keeps his kindled light:
Against the dark our Saviour's face is bright.

11

Reading Milton

I am preparing a lecture on Milton; but sometimes I think one shouldn't lecture on Milton at all – one should simply read him to people out loud, and let that beautiful sonorous poetry, that harmonious interplay between sense and sound, work its original magic on the listener.

My lecture will, I hope, be helpful, will open up some allusions, draw attention to some felicities of language, offer an interpretation that might commend the poem to the contemporary reader. But any sympathetic, resonant and metrically attuned reading is also an interpretation, and perhaps a better one; for it doesn't obtrude the lecturer's particular ideas on the reader. Rather, it leaves space for Milton's language to rouse its own, perhaps more apt and intimate, associations from somewhere deep within the listener, from depths in them that, until that moment, they didn't know existed.

This is all the more important because, compared with his immense popularity with ordinary readers in the eighteenth and nineteenth centuries, Milton's reputation and popularity have dwindled. Paradoxically, this is precisely because of the sheer weight of academic debate and interpretation which has been foisted upon him by professional scholars.

You cannot buy an edition of Milton now which is not bristling with learned footnotes. I have one in which, on some pages, there are barely four lines of the actual poem struggling up from underneath three-quarters of a page of annotation and commentary. People now assume that Milton is only for specialists. Yet, once, he was rated second only to Shakespeare, and even in a household with scarcely any other books, *Paradise Lost* would be there next to *The Pilgrim's Progress* and the Bible.

The one scholarly book that really helped me was C. S. Lewis's slim volume *A Preface to 'Paradise Lost'*, which was just that: a preface that really made you want to turn to the text. One of the most original things that Lewis says in that book is that, whereas it is a commonplace to speak of the majestic organ music of Milton's grand style, to suggest that the English language itself was his instrument and that he really pulled out all the stops, that's not quite true.

If Milton is an organist, Lewis says, then it is not so much the language that is his instrument as you yourself, your innermost heart and soul. When he appears to be describing paradise, what he is really doing, according to Lewis, is not so much describing as evoking a buried memory: he is 'pulling out the Paradisal stop in you'. It is your own deepest imagination that is playing the music and summoning the images.

I think that this is even truer than Lewis suggests. It is true not just of the passage that he analyses, but of the whole poem, and is clearly Milton's intention from the outset. Indeed, in the astonishing invocation of the Holy Spirit which opens his poem, Milton says as much. He evokes the two primal acts of creation in Genesis: the first '*Fiat lux*', the original illumination, and then the raising up of the firmament, and prays for those two primal acts, enlightening and raising, to happen within the poet and his reader:

> … What in me is dark
> Illumine, what is low raise and support;
> That to the height of this great Argument
> I may assert Eternal Providence,
> And justify the ways of God to men.

This poem, Milton is suggesting, is not just about what happened out there and back then, but about what can happen in here and right now.

12

Love and the Martyr

As we approach St Valentine's Day, I have noticed the usual flurry of online posts from 'knowledgeable' Christians smugly correcting everyone else for misunderstanding St Valentine. 'What', they ask, 'has this early Roman martyr, who was clubbed to death and beheaded, to do with all the cards, and flowers, the sentimental indulgences of Valentine's Day?'

I always feel that, in this superior finger-pointing, this self-righteous pleasure in pulling the rug out from under other people's pleasures and traditions, there is something of the same censorious and nit-picking spirit that led the Puritans to ban Christmas because there is no evidence that Jesus was born on 25 December.

Needless to say, I am entirely on the side of immemorial custom rather than the latest sceptical speculation, and, like all poets, my instinct is to 'print the legend'.

It is true that there is no evidence of an association between St Valentine and romantic love until the fourteenth century, and it was, of course, a poet, our own Geoffrey Chaucer, who made the link, in *The Parlement of Foules*, composed in about 1375. The poem refers to 14 February as the day when birds (and people) come together to find a mate. When Chaucer wrote 'For this was sent on Seynt Valentyne's day, Whan every foul cometh ther to choose his mate,' he may have invented an excellent tradition.

But he may also have been right. Why should this martyr be the saint of love? Some of the early legends seem very apt for just such an association: that he healed his jailer's blind daughter, and sent her a message signed 'your Valentine'; that, as a priest, he defied the order of Emperor Claudius and secretly performed Christian weddings, allowing the husbands involved to escape conscription into the pagan army.

This legend claims that soldiers were sparse at that time; so this was an inconvenience to the Emperor, and, of course, a way of resisting the whole odious imperial agenda. The same account mentions that, 'to remind them of their vows and God's love, Saint Valentine is said to have cut hearts from parchment', giving them to these couples as a memento not only of their love for each other, but of the love of Christ, whose own heart was pierced for them.

In the end, I thought that the best way to answer the naysayers was to take a leaf out of Chaucer's book, and write a poem of my own:

St Valentine

Why should this martyr be the saint of love?
A quiet man of unexpected courage,
A celibate who celebrated marriage,
An ageing priest with nothing left to prove,
He loved the young and made their plight his cause.
He called for fruitfulness, not waste in wars,
He found a sure foundation, stood his ground,
And gave his life to guard the love he'd found.
Why should this martyr be our Valentine?
Perhaps because he kept his covenant,
Perhaps because, with prayer still resonant,
He pledged the Bridegroom's love in holy wine,
Perhaps because the echo of his name
Can kindle love again to living flame.

13

Thank You for Waiting

'Thank you for waiting. Your call is important to us. Please hold the line and we will answer your call as soon as possible. Thank you for waiting.' And so the inane, surely inhuman, computer voice cycles on as the slow minutes tick towards the hour. 'Thank you for waiting. Your call is important to us …'

I might almost be hypnotised, carried into some contemplative state, by the phone's repetitive mantra, were it not for its randomly interruption by little loops of vapid soft-rock music, whose distorted guitars are distorted still further by my inadequate telephone speaker. But now a pause! A click! Will somebody answer? No, it's back to 'Thank you for waiting …'

I soon find myself imagining a new production of *Waiting for Godot*: the house-lights dim, and light comes up on the empty stage with its single barren tree; the audience leans forward in expectation; nothing happens. The minutes tick by. Then, from all around the auditorium, a voice intones: 'Thank you for waiting, your call is important to us …'

Eventually, Estragon and Vladimir appear in their shabby tramps' clothes and begin the compulsive cycle of their despairing, witty, tragi-comic dialogue. 'Let's go,' Estragon says. 'We can't,' Vladimir replies. 'Why not?' Estragon asks. 'We're waiting for Godot.' Silence. They stare at the pitiful tree. A cheery voice on the Tannoy says: 'Thank you for waiting, your call is important to us. Please hold the line and you will be answered as soon as possible. Alternatively, you can visit our website on www.godot.com …'

Estragon and Vladimir bang their heads against the tree, and its last few sad leaves fall to the stage.

But even that fantasy, that little diversion, soon fades, and, once again, pacing my room, I'm confronted by my complete failure in the virtue of patience, notwithstanding that I once played the part of Lucky in a student production of *Waiting for Godot*, and had to wait, holding two heavy suitcases (full of sand), through nearly the whole of the second act, before delivering the opening words of my one, wild, disjointed speech: 'Given the existence of a personal God … who loves us dearly … for reasons unknown …'

But, now, as I remember that speech, reciting it against the telephone's incessant verbiage, I also remember that I do, indeed, have a personal God who loves me dearly; and so, at last, and for the first time in that long day, I turn to him in prayer. And there he is, 'expecting me', as George Herbert says.

There he is, in all his infinite patience and compassion, waiting, waiting for me to turn to him, waiting for me to share my frustrations, to tell him my sorrows, to trust my life and time to him again. My speakerphone still babbles on, but, in the absence of Godot, God himself has come. I turn to him at last, in relief, in grace, and I say to him, with all my heart and soul: 'Thank you for waiting.'

14

Above and Beneath the Floorboards

I walk each morning through a lovely little patch of wood-land known as Sadlers Wood. On its upper ridge is a fine plantation of tall Scots pines whose high green tops would swish and sway alarmingly in the recent gales, and make a great rushing noise like an oncoming sea.

Walking warily in the strange calm beneath them, one could almost imagine one were underwater looking up at the storm above, rather as Ringo imagined himself in the Beatles' song 'Octopus's Garden'. But, for all the surge and movement of their evergreen crowns, their lovely straight stems and deep roots stayed stable and strong. It is a well-maintained wood, and one sees, in cut trees and neatly piled logs, with the lovely resinous scent of the fresh-cut wood, the careful thinning that has kept the remaining trees healthy and given them the light and space to grow so well.

In this past week, I have come home from the pine- and resin-scented woods to the scent and sight of yet more freshly cut pine, because two skilled workmen are laying down a floor of reclaimed pine boards in our new exten-sion. It is fascinating to watch them at work, cutting and trimming the planks to fit, laying them snugly alongside one another, and fastening them into place.

Seeing the work in progress, and all the hidden crafts-manship and skill that goes into it, suddenly put me in mind of something that I once heard Seamus Heaney say, 20 years ago, when I had the joy of interviewing him about the Wilfred Owen Poetry Award, which he had just won. He was talking about the craftsmanship, metrical brilliance and sheer beauty of Owen's poetry. He quoted the opening lines of 'Anthem for Doomed Youth':

What passing-bells for these who die as cattle?
– Only the monstrous anger of the guns.
Only the stuttering rifles' rapid rattle
Can patter out their hasty orisons.

Heaney marvelled at the sheer music of those lines, their intricate patterning of sound and sense, and then he said: 'I think the prosodic elements of a line, the assonance and euphony, and rhythm, are like the joists and bedding under a floorboard. You don't see them; they don't obtrude, but, because they are there, the board has the response and stability to bear its load. So it is with poetry. I think the greater the weight of grief a line is asked to bear, the more deftly and musically it must be under-sprung; for it is the beauty which helps us bear the grief.'

How right he was, and how true that is of his own poetry, those beautifully crafted pieces that helped his own nation, and all of us, to bear our burdens.

I reflected, too, on how often Heaney's poetry pays attention to the faithful craft and artistry of the people among whom he lived, with poems to celebrate the skills of the blacksmith and the thatcher, and the skills of digging turf, and digging and peeling potatoes – all these crafts lifted and transfigured by his poetry into something more than themselves.

Even as I return to my desk and take up my pen, I can hear the workmen still laying that floor, and can only hope that the lines of my poetry will be faired as truly and under-girded as firmly as that beautiful pine floor.

15

Nashotah House

Shrove Tuesday found me in the snowy wastes of Wisconsin – fortunately not out on the wind-swept prairies themselves, or on the frozen lakes; for there was an ice storm moving in for the start of Lent, and I wouldn't have survived exposure long, even in the tattered old tweed greatcoat that I was so glad I had brought with me.

No, I was warmed and well ensconced in Nashotah House, a little corner of the Midwest that is for ever Oxford. This seminary was founded in 1842, and carried the impulse, aesthetics and theology of the Oxford Movement to what was then a fairly wild frontier. There are still some original wooden buildings that go back to those days, but, later in the nineteenth century, they built a fine stone chapel in a style that has become known, rather happily, as 'Prairie Gothic', and a lovely cloister, which would not be out of place in an Oxford college, however strange it looks to English eyes, situated by a frozen lake and visited sometimes by stray deer from the woods and occasional flocks of wild turkeys.

I was there to lead an Ash Wednesday retreat, and to preach at a BCP eucharist, which was liturgically indistinguishable from any eight-o'clock service in England, except that the responses were voiced not by an elderly congregation seated as decently far apart from one another as they could manage, but by a strong cohort of young seminarians, both men and women, all dressed in their black cassocks and entering into the liturgy with great gusto.

The other interesting thing, which I later discovered from the Dean, was that they are drawn, pretty much 50–50, from both The Episcopal Church and the Anglican Church in North America. So, these two mutually severed branches of the original Anglican family, who are in so many parts of the States scarcely on speaking terms and still suing one another, are here, at least, forming unlikely friendships and, in turn, being formed together for priestly ministry – something that I take to be a sign of, at least, a little hope for the future.

The suite, just off the cloister, in which they housed me for my stay is wonderfully named Lambeth West. On the wall of my bedroom was a glorious photograph of Archbishop Michael Ramsey, wearing a big wide stetson, his cassock girded with a Western belt. He looks completely happy. I felt that, at the moment when that photo was taken, an English schoolboy's cowboy fantasy was being fulfilled.

The morning of Shrove Tuesday was marked, I am glad to say, by pancake races round the cloister, much as I have seen them in Cambridge – a fine sight: fit young people, their cassocks flying, their pancakes flipping, and great roars of encouragement from all the onlookers. The evening had more of an American flavour, themed as Mardi Gras, and that last pre-Lenten meal came out in steaming bowls of New Orleans-style Jambalaya, washed down with locally brewed beer.

Ash Wednesday, in contrast, was a day of complete prayer and fasting, the fast only broken mid-afternoon by hot cross buns. I was impressed by both the exuberance and the asceticism, and particularly by the way in which they could move seamlessly from the one to the other; for it has always been the Church's wisdom both that there should be a feast before a fast, and that the long fast of Lent should be followed by the great feast of Easter. Each informs and intensifies the other.

I'm back in Blighty now, but I was glad to have glimpsed something a little deeper and more grounded than the stereotype of a polarised American Church and society about which we so often hear.

16

Remembering the Ash

As we approach Ash Wednesday, I find, with a mixture of regret and relief, that I need no longer worry about preparing the ashes for the service. That is finally someone else's responsibility. I would always leave it to the last minute, and then have to ask myself: have I still got any of last Lent's palm crosses to burn? Can I remember how to do it? Will I set off the college fire alarm again?

I well remember the first Ash Wednesday of my priestly ministry, when I was informed by a very efficient and deeply liturgical churchwarden that I must make the ash by burning the old Palm Sunday crosses and then, to bind it, mix it with a little of the oil, blessed on the previous Maundy Thursday. Happily, she had retained stocks of both, but I soon discovered that the little crosses didn't burn very easily at all. They were almost impossible to light, and I ended up burning my fingers on my Zippo.

I did consider dowsing them with the very last of the Christmas brandy, thus adding yet another layer of complexity to the interweaving of the liturgical year, and, at the same time, minimising my temptations in Lent. But my hand was stayed by wiser heads. The thing to do, I was told, was to put the old palm crosses on a baking tray and heat them in the oven until they were completely dried out, and then they would light more easily and burn completely.

Thus I learned that oven gloves, as well as cassock-albs and cinctures, were to be part of any new priest's accoutrements. Anyway, it was all managed, in the nick of time, and I found that first ashing service to be deeply moving, especially when I knelt and was myself ashed by my long-suffering churchwarden.

It's a curious thing that we should use ash as a sign of repentance and renewal; surely it is nothing but the detritus of destruction. And yet it is so much more. Its roots are deep in scripture, in all those Old Testament passages that speak of 'repenting in dust and ashes'. Sprinkling ashes on one's head was a sign of mourning and grief – the opposite of the oil of gladness. But there is deeper wisdom still in the tradition of ashing; for the ash that is left after purging fires is itself a fertiliser, a life-enabler, a source of new growth.

Perhaps, in the current ecological crisis, ash has acquired yet another layer of meaning. Both the fire and the ash are not only signs of our personal mortality and our need for repentance and renewal, but also reminders of the wider destruction that we have inflicted on God's world and on our fellow creatures – on the whole web of life into which God has woven us and for which he also cares. Much of this was in my mind when, more than a decade ago, I wrote my sonnet for Ash Wednesday:

Receive this cross of ash upon your brow
Brought from the burning of Palm Sunday's cross;
The forests of the world are burning now
And you make late repentance for the loss.
But all the trees of God would clap their hands,
The very stones themselves would shout and sing,
If you could covenant to love these lands
And recognise in Christ their lord and king.
He sees the slow destruction of those trees,
He weeps to see the ancient places burn,
And still you make what purchases you please
And still to dust and ashes you return.
But Hope could rise from ashes even now
Beginning with this sign upon your brow.

17

Launch Out into the Deep

'Launch out into the deep.' I love these words of Jesus to Peter. Having turned Peter's boat into a makeshift pulpit for a while, Jesus turns to his new friend and says, as it were, 'Now for the adventure of a lifetime – launch out into the deep!' I love these words as much for what they mean literally as for all that they mean symbolically.

I have always loved boats, and, when I was a little boy and was read the stories of Jesus from an illustrated Bible, I was very fond of the picture that went with this one. A shoreside scene: the people gathered, the fishing nets piled and drying at the side, one or two other fishing boats bobbing in the offing, and, in the centre, full of glorious detail, Peter's boat, with Jesus on board.

It was a magnificent double-ender, carvel built and beautifully fared, with a high prow and a strong-looking stern post. Jesus stood beneath its single mast, and, above it, a cross spar still with its furled sail suggested the adventures still to come – and, had I eyes to see it, foreshadowed the cross. Even when my parents could not be persuaded to read the story again, I used to ask for the book, so that I could keep gazing at the picture and take it all in.

So, I was thrilled when it was reported, in early 1986, that just such a boat, dating from the first century, had been discovered, comparatively well preserved, in the muddy lakebed of Galilee. I was all the more thrilled because that was the year when Maggie and I visited the Holy Land, and we saw the excavations: the dark ribs and planking of a vessel just the size and shape of the one that I had seen in my children's Bible. They had made a little model of how it would look once it was restored, and it was all just as I had imagined.

It was all there in my mind, too, when I wrote the opening quatrain of my sonnet on the call of the disciples:

He calls us all to step aboard his ship,
Take the adventure on this morning's wing,
Raise sail with him, launch out into the deep,
Whatever storms or floods are threatening.

The phrase 'launch out into the deep' has been stirring again in my mind for the more secular reason that, with the first tentative signs of spring, now February is past, my mind, like the mind of any sailor, has turned to finding the right day to launch my boat – to get her out from her winter sleep under tarpaulins in the barn of a genial farmer in Repps, and get her afloat again and down to her moorings at Ranworth. There will be preparations first, of course: a spring clean, a little varnishing, going through all her rigging, checking that everything is shipshape, and then waiting for the right day, with wind and weather set fair.

Naturally, there will be a prayer of blessing, too, and something to drink for captain and crew, on the day.

In my case, Jesus won't be telling me to launch out into the deep, as most of the Broads are shallow enough to stand in; but, in faith, I'll still have Jesus on board with me, just as Peter did.

18

That Morning

I was going to write about that morning I came down to the River Dart, down to the splashing, darting, sparkling waters that Ted Hughes called his 'champagne river'. I was going to write about coming down, on a crisp February morning, the air brightened and cleansed from the storms, down from the folds of an ancient combe, in the company of a renowned Devonian storyteller, down to the very spot that Hughes loved to fish. I was going to tell you how, standing above the surge of the river, the endless beautiful reshaping of its currents and cataracts, its sheer continuance of form amid the constant change of its content, I had recalled the opening lines of Hughes's beautiful poem 'That Morning':

> We came where the salmon were so many
> So steady, so spaced, so far-aimed
> On their inner map ...

I was going to write about how I, too, for a moment, felt the same sense of epiphany as Hughes had felt, standing there 'in the pollen light', 'lifted ... towards some dazzle of blessing'.

I was going to write that; but when I came home to put pen to paper, it seemed as though the world had changed and darkened, and that Devon morning, only two days before, was just a distant dream. For I had come home to the news of war, to the missiles flying and the tanks rolling across Ukraine, the tyrant's fist crushing and closing on a nation's freedom. How could I write, in such a moment, about poetry and fishing?

And then, as from some half-remembered depth, came the words of C. S. Lewis, words from a sermon that he preached in Oxford in December of 1939, as tanks rolled across Europe and frightened and bewildered students gathered in the church of St Mary the Virgin, asking themselves the very questions that Lewis posed in the opening of his sermon, variants of the question I was asking myself now: 'What is the use', Lewis asked from the pulpit, 'of beginning a task which we have so little chance of finishing? … why should we – indeed how can we – continue to take an interest in these placid occupations when the lives of our friends and the liberties of Europe are in the balance? Is it not like fiddling while Rome burns?'

So, I returned to that sermon, later published under the title 'Learning in War-Time', and found it to be as full of wisdom for our moment in history as it was for his. At the core of it is a call to do everything as on a precipice, to do everything only because it is intrinsically worth doing, and all the more so because it might be the last thing we do; to do everything, from crafting a poem, to defending a city, to the glory of God: 'The war creates no absolutely new situation: it simply aggravates the permanent human situation so that we can no longer ignore it. Human life has always been lived on the edge of a precipice. Human culture has always had to exist under the shadow … [We] propound mathematical theorems in beleaguered cities, conduct metaphysical arguments in condemned cells, make jokes on scaffolds, discuss the last new poem whilst advancing to the walls of Quebec …'

So I resume my original task, letting poetry lighten even the darkest hour, and share with you the end of Hughes's great poem:

So we found the end of our journey.
So we stood, alive in the river of light,
Among the creatures of light, creatures of light.

19

Norfolk Pamments

Just in front of the little writing shed in our garden, we have laid a small terrace of old, reclaimed Norfolk pamments, in the hope that when and if the weather clears, I can sit outside the hut (called the Temple of Peace, more in hope than expectation), enjoy the sun and write a poem or two. But I shall enjoy the pamments as well; for they are a uniquely Norfolk thing.

Pamments are buff, red or reddish-brown terracotta tiles, made locally from sand and clay, just as it comes from the earth, with all its singular characteristics and 'imperfections' – though these supposed 'imperfections' include little fragments of glittering quartz, or even beautiful fossils. No two pamments are quite the same; for the mud from which they are made is not homogeneous. Set together in a floor or terrace, they seem, between them, to summon subtly different patterns on different days in different lights. Yet many might walk over them without ever noticing.

I first became aware of them because the church in Linton, Cambridgeshire, of which Maggie was Rector, had a floor patterned with red and buff pamments, and, when there was any need for repair or restoration, someone from the church would go up to north Norfolk and take a tour of reclamation yards to look out for some 'good old pamments' to patch the floor in the nave.

There is, in fact, still one Norfolk firm that continues to make them by hand, using the same techniques and local materials as they have been made with for centuries. A mother-and-daughter team, down in Pulham Market, they take as their slogan, I am happy to say, 'Good as old'. They make no bones about the homely and humble nature of their raw materials, and say on their website: 'We are proud of our skill at transforming mud into tiles.'

Contemplating the pamment floor in St Mary's, Linton, I sometimes wondered whether I should write a different version of George Herbert's excellent poem 'The Church Floor'. Herbert was, of course, writing about the rather more elaborate floors in 'square and speckled stone' which he and Nicholas Ferrar were laying at their own expense at Leighton Bromswold and Little Gidding. There, the pattern was made by chequered black and white stone:

> Mark you the floore? that square & speckled stone,
> Which looks so firm and strong,
> Is *Patience*:
> And th' other black and grave, where with each one
> Is checker'd all along,
> *Humilitie.*

Were I to make a pamment poem, it would not be about our own patterning, or about the fine marble mentioned later in Herbert's poem. Rather, it would be about the humble local clay – or let us call it mud – from which, in Genesis, even we are made.

It would be about how 'singular characteristics' and even 'imperfections' can be taken up by Christ the craftsman into a beautiful, variegated, purposeful pattern. It would have something to say about how those odd beauties in our neighbours, all of us tiles in the church, are sometimes overlooked and trodden under, though really they support us all …

Perhaps, if the weather improves and I can sit by my pamment terrace at the Temple of Peace, I'll have a chance to write it.

20

Remembering Yeats in a Time of War

It is strange, but somehow heartening, as I begin each morning walk, to turn from the dire sounds of warfare transmitted to us live on the *Today* programme by those incredibly brave BBC journalists, to turn from that dissonant radio soundscape, into our local woods, alive with lovely birdsong, and see the birds themselves flitting between the trees and bushes, beginning to build their nests.

Our minds are full of the human distress, the heart-rending testimonies of mothers and children which we hear daily, and yet, walking through the woods as the birds build their nests, oblivious of our turmoil, I also wondered about the other living communities of Ukraine: the birds, the bees and insects, the wild animals, the fields of golden sunflowers, the whole realm of nature recoiling, and perhaps one day recovering from a human, and inhuman, war. Has 'the sparrow still found her a house and the swallow a nest' in some bombed-out church or cathedral?

Suddenly, I found myself remembering 'The Stare's [starling's] Nest By My Window', that poignant poem from Yeats's *Meditations in Time of Civil War*. Writing by the window of his crumbling Norman tower, itself the monument of previous invasions, and writing at a time of new war, when, as he says later in the poem, 'they trundled down the road, That dead young soldier in his blood,' Yeats sees the nest-building, and, even amid destruction, finds an emblem of hope and nurture:

The bees build in the crevices
Of loosening masonry, and there
The mother birds bring grubs and flies.

My wall is loosening; honey-bees
Come build in the empty house of the stare.

The very next verse, so apt for Yeats's time, could be a report from the front lines of our own, could be spoken as much by the besieged in Kyiv as by those who hear their pleas on an English radio – both left bewildered and seemingly helpless by this sudden cataclysm:

We are closed in, and the key is turned
On our uncertainty; somewhere
A man is killed, or a house burned,
Yet no clear fact to be discerned:
Come build in the empty house of the stare.

And still the spring unfolds. Though we are closed in, though 'the key is turned, on our uncertainty,' the mother birds still feed their young, the bees build in the crevices, and that same impulse, in the heart of the one life that we share with these creatures, must work in us, to love and nurture, to build again even amid ruins.

Yeats ends his poem with a confession – a confession of those ruinous and brutal fantasies that fuel human violence and warfare, and themselves war against our truest impulses, the ones that come from what Yeats once called 'the deep heart's core'. And so he writes his final verse:

We had fed the heart on fantasies,
The heart's grown brutal from the fare;
More substance in our enmities
Than in our love; O honeybees,
Come build in the empty house of the stare.

Recalling those words, I find myself in prayer, not only for all the mothers of Ukraine who are seeking, like the birds, to nurture their young, but also for all those who, like the indefatigable honey bees, must begin the work again of building amid the ruins a new place of community, something that will yield honey, the sweet nurture of love, even amid such bitterness.

21

Merlin's Barrow

I had an extraordinary experience the other evening. I had gone down to stay in Marlborough for a few days, to preach in the chapel and to give some lectures and seminars to the sixth-formers at the College there. I arrived at dusk, and was almost immediately whisked off to attend a school concert, which was excellent.

As we walked back afterwards, with the long Victorian chapel on our left, I looked over to my right, peering through the gloaming, and it was as though some veil of time had been lifted and I was gazing into another age. Instead of the Victorian school buildings and dormitories I was expecting, I saw, rising before me, a great green hill, clearly an earthwork mound or barrow, perfectly shaped, with a glimmering white path spiralling up to its summit, and ancient yews clinging to its sides and around its crown. A little mist drifted by in the half dark, and I felt that I could have been gazing on some corner of Middle-earth, or some fairy mound. I half expected the fair folk to issue from that hill, or to be present at the Hosting of the Sidhe.

'Am I seeing things?' I asked my host. 'Ah,' he said, 'did you not know? That is Merlin's Barrow, the *MerleBerge*, as they called Marlborough in the Domesday Book, but of course it's much older than even Merlin – I'll tell you about it in the morning.'

He was as good as his word – and better; for I not only learned the extraordinary history of 'the mound', as the school calls it, but was allowed to take the spiral path that encircles the mound six times before it reaches the summit.

Historians, unsurprisingly, don't take the Merlin legend seriously, notwithstanding the town's motto 'Ubi nunc sapientis ossa Merlini' ('Where now are the bones of Merlin the wise'). But the history is almost more remarkable than the legend. At first, it was assumed that the mound was simply the motte of the Norman castle that had once stood there, which would take it back to the 1100s, although it is far larger than any motte need have been. But some historians wondered whether it might be older still – whether it might have been there already, before the Normans came.

And then, just ten years ago, came an astonishing discovery. Core samples were taken from right through the mound for carbon dating, and 'Merlin's Barrow' was found to date from 2400 BC! It had stood there millennia before the age of Arthur and Merlin. It turns out to be a Neolithic monument contemporary with Stonehenge, and with its bigger sister five miles west along the Kennet at Silbury Hill, which is Europe's largest man-made prehistoric hill.

As I climbed up the spiralling chalk path to the summit of the mound that morning, I could see a white horse carved on the flanks of the valley and the sun glinting on the clear waters of the Kennet, the pure chalk stream that rises at Silbury and runs eastward towards the rising sun, down through Marlborough and past this mound.

Even at this date, so remote from its making, I could sense, in that magical alignment of earth, water and the light of the sun, something of the numinous and sacred geometry marked out by our remote ancestors. Then I gazed from the mound across to the chapel where I would be telling the story of how the Light of Life came to earth, and revealed himself as the true source, offering us a fountain rising in us to eternal life, and I was glad to turn from one sacred place to another.

22

On the Thames

I have been out on the Thames, or 'London River', as the old Norfolk wherrymen used to call it. It's always a pleasure, and often an awe-inspiring experience, to be on that great river; for it carries in its tides and currents, and along the arcs and curves of its course, so much history – and, indeed, pre-history.

If one is even slightly aware of what T. S. Eliot called 'the present moment of the past', then even ten minutes on the Thames is almost too intense an experience; and I had the pleasure of being out and about on it for the best part of a day. It was low tide when I walked down the steep gangway, with my son and my old friend Sean, to board one of the Uber Boat Clippers, with our all-day passes.

Already, the indefatigable 'mudlarks' were out, picking their way along banks that the receding tide revealed; for, buried and sometimes surfacing unexpectedly in those banks are all the oddments, thrown away or lost, from more than 2,000 years of Thameside life; and the mudlarks, as these beachcombers call themselves, find and treasure so much that was once lost and cast off: old clay pipes, coins from many reigns right back to Roman times, glass beads, old rings, and sometimes more precious bits of jewellery – earrings slipped to the tide on some moonlit Elizabethan tryst, all buried and revealed again to those with sharp eyes and good luck.

But, as we were ferried down the Thames under Tower Bridge and past the Tower itself, making our way to Greenwich and the *Cutty Sark*, the buildings along either bank were also witness at once to change and continuity. Between the modern towers of steel and glass in the City, and the other clutch of them down at Canary Wharf, are all the old warehouses, docks and wharfs of the Victorian Thameside, where goods from all over the world were brought upriver in tall ships and hoisted up on cranes into warehouses. Some of the old cranes and gantries are still there on the buildings, but the warehouses themselves are all converted into bijou flats and studios.

And, then, squeezed in between those larger buildings are little sixteenth-century inns hanging on, in spite of everything, their history in their names: the Mayflower, the Prospect of Whitby.

As we passed by some of the older warehouses, which once belonged to the East India Company, Sean remembered and recited a poem that John Masefield wrote, as Laureate, in 1914, after a visit to such a warehouse:

> … you showed me nutmegs and nutmeg husks,
> Ostrich feathers and elephant tusks,
> Hundreds of tons of costly tea …
> And choice port wine from a bright glass fount,
> You showed, for a most delightful hour,
> The wealth of the world, and London's power.

That last line has an ambivalence that we feel even more deeply now than Masefield may have felt it then: 'The wealth of the world, and London's power.' As we reappraise our colonial history, we are much more aware of the cruelty and inhumanity running through that power that drew so much of the wealth of the world to London, from the exploitation of enslaved labour to the setting of unfair and extortionate terms of 'trade', and the gunboat diplomacy that enforced those terms. And one thinks of the opium wars; for the long list in Masefield's poem also includes 'a myriad drugs which disagree'.

Yet, all that history to be retold, at times to be repented, lies not just in the books and universities, but is also, as every mudlark knows, waiting to be discovered right under our feet.

23

A Golden Era

One advantage of moving house is that you see all your old things with new eyes. Books are in a different order and on different shelves; pictures hang on new walls in different rooms; and you begin to see them, quite literally, in a new light. It is as though you've acquired them all afresh.

So it is that, when I pause, a little breathless from climbing our rather steep stairs, I can enjoy, close-up and at eye level, a beautiful painting, looking out from Ruskin's house Brantwood, across Coniston Water to the fells and the Old Man of Coniston. But it is a painting of far more than the glorious view that any camera might have captured: it is a painting of the weather, the atmosphere, the astonishing interplay of darkness and light, the sheer feel of those northern fells and of something more in the gleams of light, in white and gold, and the tiny patches of deep and distant blue which shimmer behind and sometimes through the dark and massy clouds, 'Which image in their bulk both lakes and shores, And mountain crags', as Coleridge writes in 'Frost at Midnight'.

And it is a painting that captures even more than that; for it seems, to me at least, to clarify something that Coleridge says in the very next lines of that poem, to show me again:

The lovely shapes and sounds intelligible
Of that eternal language, which thy God
Utters, who from eternity doth teach
Himself in all, and all things in himself.

The work is by Daniel L. Cooper, in charcoal and mixed media, and it is a miracle to me that the charcoal that they used to burn on those fells (as I learned from my childhood readings of Arthur Ransome, so many of whose stories are set in this very place) should be able so completely, in the hands of an artist, to express the very spirit of the landscape from which it was drawn.

Among the other media in the work are just the faintest traces of gold and white under the clouds, hinting at the sun we cannot see. I scarcely saw those hints and glints of gold where the painting hung in our old house: they hid themselves and just left the suggestion of light. But here, in the new house in Norfolk, standing a little closer, I am transported from the East Anglian reeds and broads to that other English wildness of the fells and lakes, transfigured in light, transfiguring the earthen media of which they are made.

The painting is called *A Golden Era*, and we saw and fell in love with it in a gallery in Brantwood itself, on holiday in the summer of 2019 – a summer that, considering the almost continuous oppression of crises since then, does indeed seem like a golden era.

And so it is that, as I stand at the top of my stairs, personal and literary memory of Ransome, Ruskin, Wordsworth and Coleridge fuses and coheres around this flat rectangle of beauty. On each encounter, it seems less like an opaque arrangement of paper and charcoal on which the light of Norfolk falls, and more like a window from which the light of Cumbria, and something more than the light of this world, streams out.

24

Cherry Blossoms

The other day, I was taken by friends on a circular walk along beautiful avenues of flowering cherry trees, their branches arching over us so that the profusion of delicate blossoms almost brushed our heads. When a gentle breeze stirred, white petals would lift and fall like little snow flurries. The trees themselves were very old, some so dark and gnarled and hollowed out by the years that it seemed a miracle that they still lived, let alone that they could greet the spring like this – that out of such an unpromising stock and stem, such finely wrought and fragile beauty could emerge.

But, if that was surprising, then so was my entire situation. I had flown out to the States to do some poetry readings at the Virginia Theological Seminary, not realising till I got there that it is situated just next to Washington, DC, and that I had arrived, happily, just in time for the Washington Cherry Blossom Festival. This is a time when people come from miles around to walk the shores of the tidal basin, beneath the hundreds of cherry trees, which were a gift from Japan more than a century ago, and have blossomed faithfully, as fresh as ever from their ageing stems, through all the dark vicissitudes, all the long struggles of the twentieth and twenty-first centuries.

There was something telling and poignant about the context: through the branches that leant out over the water, I could gaze across at the Jefferson Memorial; and, when our walk round the shores eventually led us to that august and classical building, I could gaze across from its marble steps directly at the White House.

And all the time we walked through the blossoms, in beautiful scenes that could have come from some nineteenth-century Japanese print, the air above us was filled with the chopping, pounding sound of low-flying military helicopters, travelling in and out to the Capitol from the Pentagon and the military bases on the Potomac. One of these helicopters, flying low and fast, my host assured me, was Marine 1, bringing the President to a meeting in the White House.

Not even among these magical scatterings of blossom could we forget that the world is in crisis. And yet these trees had stood through so much, must remember so much, the two world wars come and gone, the political and cultural crises, rolling and roiling through the capital. They had blossomed on through it all. I thought of Basho's famous verse:

How many, many things
They call to mind
These cherry-blossoms!

I thought, too, here in the centre of one of the great world powers, about power itself. The powerful helicopters, flying menacingly low, were one kind of power: power from above, power to dominate, the power that turns out sometimes to be no more than the power to destroy, a power that often destroys itself. And then I thought of the extraordinary hidden power, the flow and force of life itself, 'the force that through the green fuse drives the flower,' as Dylan Thomas said. The gentle power that could still bring blossoms from a tree so old that its trunk was almost completely hollow, and its one stooping branch, held up with props, but still flowering in beauty one hundred years on.

I paused to pray beside that tree, and found myself remembering another tree, raised in darkness and despair 2,000 years ago, from which blossomed a love and power that still transforms the world, still gives us hope.

25

Advice

I returned to Cambridge the other day, to preach at Trinity College. It was a joy to revisit the city where I have spent so much of my life. I tried, in all my Cambridge years, not to take the place for granted, still to be astonished by its beauty, its history, the long continuous succession of its academic and literary life. Moving away gave me some perspective on what I had been privileged to share, and returning renewed my sense of wonder.

There is a particular pleasure in walking through the gates of Trinity into that glorious, spacious Great Court. There is something significant about such surprising spaciousness set within the college itself: a roofless space held open to the sun and stars by a curtilage of buildings, which are themselves smaller and roofed and enclosed.

So it is also with the life of the mind: the academic institutions, the schools and the universities are like the buildings that surround and make up that Great Court, each with its own style and history, but each also limited and defined by the walls and roofs of its particular discipline and tradition.

But they are not there simply to contain and organise the knowledge of the past, all that has been accumulated so far. They are there to preserve, to hold between them, and to defend that far greater space that also stands, like the Trinity Great Court, open, empty, roofless, apparently useless. But that open, empty space, unroofed, open to light from the furthest star, that space is the space of the mind itself in all its life and growth, ready to be explored and expanded further, open to every new thought and possibility – a place, as they say in Cambridge, for 'blue-sky thinking'.

Governments and administrations are, of course, always trying to fill up that open space with a clutter of temporary practicalities, measurable objectives and predetermined 'learning outcomes', as though a university were just a factory for churning out economically productive technocrats. But, still, in spite of all, the Great Court lies open and empty, both in its outward and visible form, and in its inward and intellectual meaning.

I was to preach the final sermon of the Lent term, and my theme, I was told, was to be the advice that I would give to my former student self, if I could travel back as I am now and speak to him. An impossible task, of course, not least because I would have to ask: 'To which of my former student selves would I be speaking?' For I came up to Cambridge thinking that I knew everything, and I left knowing that I knew almost nothing. I came up a closed-minded atheist, and left an open-minded Christian. I came up, as I thought, already an ardent poet, and left knowing that I was a mere beginner in the humble craft of fitting words together.

Also, it occurred to me that even if I were to travel back as a grey-haired 65-year-old, collar my 19-year-old self, and sit him down for my supposedly wise words, was there any chance that he would listen? He had already ignored so much sage advice from his elders and betters.

So, I thought it more practical to ask in my sermon: what advice would all my growing, changing, student selves give to me now? I think that it would amount to something like this: 'Don't settle, don't get stuck, don't rest on laurels. Keep growing, keep thinking, keep asking, keep changing.' It is advice that might be summed up in St Paul's words: 'Do not be conformed to this world but rather be ye transformed by the renewal of your mind …'

26

A Minor Exorcism

I have a dread of underground car parks. It's more than mild claustrophobia, more than a natural reaction against the grim brutalist architecture, the cold and forbidding slabs of concrete that always feature in such places. It's a foreboding sense of something sinister, the feeling that I'm in the sort of place which has witnessed or will witness the violent denouement of some hideous gangster film.

I am happy to report, however, that this irrational dread has now had its proper liturgical cleansing, its own little exorcism, and that, rather surprisingly, this moment of deliverance occurred in an underground car park in Dallas.

Let me explain. I was in Dallas for a performance of 'Ordinary Saints', the composition combining poetry, painting and music, on which I collaborated with the painter Bruce Herman and the composer J. A. C. Redford. We were there for the whole weekend, taking part in services, giving talks and leading a mini-retreat, as well as for the actual performance; and the day of the retreat concluded with a beautiful sung compline, which I was asked to lead, and which included Orlando Gibbons's setting of the Nunc Dimittis and Palestrina's 'Sicut cervus'.

Then came the adventure. Although the church has a beautiful auditorium and sanctuary, the director of music felt that the best acoustic for this compline was to be found in the church's underground car park. He had made this discovery, he told me, when his children had been delighted with the way the car park amplified their squeals and shouts. Then he tried singing, and was delighted with the result. 'There's no crude echo or "slapback"', he told me, 'just a wonderful bloom and expansion of the sound, a rich exfoliation.

It's going to be perfect for the Palestrina; in fact, it's just like King's College Chapel.' Perhaps the first and last time that that miracle of fan vaulting, delicate tracery and light has been compared to an underground car park!

So, at the appointed time, I robed, and led the choir and congregation down into a place which, until then, had made me shudder. We were greeted by ushers as we entered, and given lighted candles. The choir formed up in a semicircle, incongruous against the backdrop of concrete ramps and grey forbidding walls, the circles of light from their candles flickering against the low ceiling. Then they drew breath, and the miracle happened, as music filled and transfigured the place:

> Music to stir and call the sleeping soul,
> And set a counterpoint to all our pain,
> To bless our senses in their very essence
> And undergird our sorrow in good ground.
> Music to summon undeserved abundance,
> Unlooked-for over-brimming, rich and strong;
> The unexpected plenitude of sound
> Becoming song.

Those words, which I had written years ago in an 'Ode to St Cecilia', came back to me as the sound of the choir so richly filled that bleak place and blessed it with beauty. It was transformed, and, as the service drew to a close, I was able to intone fully and finally the prayer I had often muttered under my breath in such places before: compline's great collect of cleansing and deliverance.

'Visit, we beseech thee, O Lord, this place, and drive from it all the snares of the enemy; may thy holy angels dwell herein to preserve us in peace, and may thy blessing be upon us evermore, through Jesus Christ our Lord. Amen.'

27

A Breath of Heaven

Both of the Easter Day appearances of the risen Christ in St John's Gospel have the kind of luminosity and depth that draws one back, again and again, over many years, always to find something new and stimulating.

As a younger man, I was always drawn to the scene at Easter dawn, which has, in Czeslaw Milosz's phrase, 'the clarity of early morning'. I loved the sudden transformation of Mary from sorrow to joy when she hears her own name on the lips of her Saviour, and her joyful sprint to tell the others, and so become, as Lancelot Andrewes says, 'an Apostle to the Apostles, an Evangelist to the Evangelists'.

But now, nearer the evening of my life, it is the evening appearance, which immediately follows it in John's narrative, that draws me in. There are the disciples, behind locked doors, not only cautious, but, frankly, fearful, notwithstanding the news that Mary had brought them that morning. And then Jesus appears in their midst, and the first word on his lips is 'Peace'. In increasingly anxious and fearful times, it is a word one is longing deeply to hear. Then comes that extraordinary moment, a kind of Pentecost before Pentecost, in which he breathes on them and says, 'Receive the Holy Spirit.'

It seems to me that there is a lovely recapitulation of the Genesis creation narrative going on here. No, not so much a recapitulation as a delicate mirroring of the moment in the garden when the Lord breathes into the clay of the first person, and makes them a living being – 'a human being fully alive', as Irenaeus says.

Indeed, it's almost a chiasmic sequence, as the New Testament mirrors and reverses the order of the Old. In Genesis, the first creation, we start with the cosmic coming of the Creator Spirit, the Spirit of God moving on the face of the deep, and then comes the personal inbreathing of the Spirit into Adam in the garden. But, in the New Testament, the ordering of the new creation, we start with this intimate, personal inbreathing of the Spirit; and then, in Acts, we have the cosmic event: the mighty rushing wind, the tongues of fire, the birth of the Church, the transformation of the world.

That moment in the upper room also took on new meaning for me in those panicky days of the first Covid lockdown. Once more, we were living in fear behind locked doors, once more everything turned on breathing. I tried to get a little of how pertinent John's vision became at that time, in this sonnet:

This Breathless Earth (John 20.19)

We bolted every door but even so
We couldn't catch our breath for very fear:
Fear of their knocking at the gate below,
Fear that they'd find and kill us even here.
Though Mary's tale had quickened all our hearts
Each fleeting hope just deepens your despair:
The panic grips again, the gasping starts,
The drowning, and the coming up for air.

Then suddenly, a different atmosphere,
A clarity of light, a strange release,
And, all unlooked for, Christ himself was there
Love in his eyes and on his lips, our peace.
So now we breathe again, sent forth, forgiven,
To bring this breathless earth a breath of heaven.

28

At a Consecration

I spent the first half of Holy Week at St Deiniol's Cathedral, Bangor, and witnessed a wonderful blending of the ancient and contemporary; or not so much a blending as a beautiful overlaying and interlapping of past and present.

The cathedral stands on the sacred ground where, in 525, St Deiniol gathered a Christian community and raised around it a hazel fence – the original 'Bangor' – for shelter and sanctuary. Eventually, he became abbot of that community, and then bishop of a diocese that has some claim to be one of the oldest in the British Isles.

I was there as a visiting poet and preacher; for the cathedral had chosen to weave my poetry in and out of some of its Holy Week services. Although I was able to read my poems only in their original English, I was thrilled to hear them also read beautifully and melodically in Welsh by the Sub-Dean, for whom Welsh is a first language. Indeed, all the services there were bilingual, moving seamlessly between the two languages; and translations were provided in the orders of service for speakers in either tongue.

The cathedral had commissioned Dr Siôn Aled, a crowned bard, to translate the full sequence of my Holy Week sonnets, from Palm Sunday to Easter dawn, producing a beautiful bilingual booklet. He made verse translations, maintaining the sonnet form, which were as much poems in their own right and language as they were 'versions' of mine.

It seemed fitting to me that they should find this new form as Welsh poems, in a place founded by St Deiniol, since it was at St Deiniol's, in Hawarden, as the wonderful Gladstone's Library was then called, that I composed them. I was able to meet and talk with Dr Aled, and thank him for his work with my poems, and also hear from him how, in the Welsh poetic tradition, there was still a strong engagement with poetic form: something which I have been trying, in a small way, to revive in English.

It was not only the beauty of translation which moved me, but also a moment of consecration. At the chrism service, and the renewal of vows for the clergy and lay ministers of the diocese, they were also dedicating and consecrating a new nave altar-table: a beautiful and simple piece of furniture, a wooden trestle table whose design evoked both a carpenter's workbench and the tables that one sees in some depictions of the Last Supper.

But here, again, the ancient and the new were interlayered; for they brought to the table, and placed within it, a little cache of the soil of Bardsey Island, the island of 20,000 saints, one of whom was St Deiniol, so that the dust of the saints carried with it the reminder of the communion of the saints invoked in the eucharist.

Best of all, though, was the line of poetry composed by the translator of my sonnets and inscribed in Welsh at the front of the altar-table. Its English translation reads: 'From the blue slate abundance flows to fill afresh our llannau's wells.' It was a beautiful evocation both of the miraculous stream flowing from the rock in Exodus, of Christ as the 'stricken rock with streaming side', and also of the slates of the Ogwen Valley and the River Adda flowing past Bangor and the 'llanau', the glades of the Celtic saints, and their abundant holy wells.

Receiving communion from that table, I felt that I had indeed come to a wellhead, a source, and, through it, once again, to the source of all things.

29

Musing on Psalm 84

During the course of this long slow spring my daily walks
with George and Zara took me past St Mary's church in
Linton, and I watched the spring open out in blossom, scat-
tering wildflowers through the churchyard, watched the
tender green leaves unfold on the lime trees, the squirrels in
the woodland patch awake from hibernation and find their
hidden stores, and everywhere in brake and bush the chorus
of birdsong and little glimpses of the birds themselves building their nests. And yet in the midst of it all that opening out
and thriving stood the church itself, locked and closed. Even
though that closure was itself an act of love and care, I always
felt a pang passing it by, and felt almost as if the building
itself were joining me in grief and longing to be open again.
And often, as I watched the birds flit past between me and
the church, those verses from Psalm 84 would come to me:
'Yea, the sparrow hath found her an house, and the swallow
a nest where she may lay her young: even thy altars, O Lord
of hosts, my King and my God.' I certainly felt the 'desire
and longing' the psalmist speaks of, to 'enter into those
courts' again.

Then the day came when we could open for 'private
prayer' and I remember with what loving care and caution
it was arranged: with the carefully spaced chairs, and the
sanitiser, and indeed a rota of church-sitters for the opening
hours to make sure everyone was safe, and keeping it safe for
others. They too, those patient church-sitters, like the spar-
rows and the swallows had found their own place in Psalm
84: 'I had rather be a door-keeper in the house of my God:
than to dwell in the tents of ungodliness.'

I make no suggestion of course as to where the 'tents of ungodliness' may be pitched these days, but I do know that when one is 'going through the vale of misery' as we all have been of late, then an open church, quiet and inviting, can indeed be, as the psalmist says, like 'a well' whose 'pools are filled with water'.

I had reached Psalm 84, in my new series of poems responding to the psalter, just at the time we were opening St Mary's again and one of the first things I did was to slip in and read the poem aloud in that lovely, resonant, holy space.

LXXXIV *Quam dilecta!*

Yahweh saves, Our God is merciful
And how I long to enter in his courts
To nestle at his altar and to dwell

With him forever. Day and night my thoughts
Are yearning towards the beauty of his temple
In 'swallow-flights of song'. For in his courts

Time is transfigured, opened out and ample,
It touches on eternity. I stay
Awhile within this church, its simple

Furnishings, and storied windows say
More to me of heaven than the pale
Abstractions of theology. A day

Spent in an empty church has been as full
Of goodness as an age elsewhere. I feel
Its peace refresh me like a holy well.

30

In King's College Chapel

Having led compline in that underground car park in Dallas whose acoustic was so generously compared to that of King's College Chapel, in Cambridge, I found myself in that very chapel only a fortnight later, attending a beautiful service of compline.

I forbear to make any direct comparisons between the sound of the two services; but the atmosphere and setting, the sense of place, the beauty of what lay before one's eyes – that is another matter. I slumped my tired body into one of those beautiful old wooden stalls, and let the continuous miracle of music and litany do its work, as George Herbert promised it would: 'Now I in you without a bodie move, Rising and falling with your wings.'

Jet-lagged as I was, I felt myself lifted by the music floating up towards the wonderful tracery of that fan-vaulted roof, and, in that lifting, I felt my soul breathe and expand.

As I contemplated that ceiling, another poem stirred in my memory, to give me words for what I was experiencing:

These lofty pillars, spread that branching roof
Self-poised, and scooped into ten thousand cells,
Where light and shade repose, where music dwells
Lingering – and wandering on as loth to die;
Like thoughts whose very sweetness yieldeth proof
That they were born for immortality.

Those last six lines of Wordsworth's sonnet, 'Inside of King's College Chapel, Cambridge', lift towards the sublime from a poem that, quite frankly, begins with the banal.

'Tax not the royal Saint with vain expense' is not a promising start. Any line that opens with 'tax' and ends with 'expense' is not likely to woo or enchant the reader.

Wordsworth, to be fair on him, was responding to a sniping account of the chapel in William Gilpin's *Picturesque Tours*, a book that Wordsworth otherwise admired. After visiting the chapel, Gilpin had written: 'Its disproportion disgusts. Such height and such length, united by such straightened parallels, hurts the eye. You feel immured. Henry the Sixth, we are told, spent twelve hundred pounds in adorning the roof. It is a pity he had not spent it in widening the walls.'

No wonder Wordsworth responded as he did:

Tax not the royal Saint with vain expense,
With ill-matched aims the Architect who planned –
Albeit labouring for a scanty band
Of white-robed Scholars only – this immense
And glorious Work of fine intelligence!

There was little sign of that 'scanty band of white-robed scholars', or, nowadays, black-robed scholars, for whom the chapel was built during that particular compline, apart from the white-surpliced choir itself; but we were, nevertheless, a gathering of scholars. I was there as part of an international colloquium on theology and the arts, and there could scarcely have been a better place for such a gathering. If ever there was a work of human art which gives outward and visible expression to the deepest mysteries with which theology is concerned, then it is the chapel in which our intellectual efforts were, on that first evening, consecrated with prayer.

And, whatever the outcome of our deliberations, when they finally find expression as a book, we can aspire only to make, like those who made that chapel, such a 'glorious Work of fine intelligence'.

31

In Brontë Country

When you walk into a pub where the four real ales on offer are called, respectively, Anne, Branwell, Charlotte and Emily, then you know you are in Brontë country. Mind you, I didn't need the ales to remind me; for I had come to the King's Arms in Haworth directly from the Brontë Parsonage Museum. So my mind was full of the brilliance, compassion and tragedy woven through the personal stories of those astonishing storytellers.

The museum is beautifully laid out, and contains many treasures – not least the desks, pens, quills, notebooks and manuscripts of Anne, Charlotte and Emily, from the tiny books that they made when they told stories to and about Branwell's toy soldiers as children, to the copies, translations and correspondence that flowed from the huge success of *Jane Eyre*.

I love standing in the studies of writers I admire, and seeing the very desks on which they wrote. It gives me a kind of happy vertigo: a sense of the finite giving rise to endlessly generative spirals of the infinite. From these small, folding desks flowed the great worlds of the novels, and not just the world of the novel as it was written, but the new world that each new reading of the novel forms in the active imagination of each new reader – all those worlds began here, generated from the single generous act of imagination, engendered faithfully with pen and quill at these little desks.

But, curiously, it was not the rooms of the successful writers that moved me most, but the room of the Brontë who died in disappointment and apparent failure: Branwell, the brilliant son and much-loved brother, on whom such great expectations were laid, and who could not, in the end, bear the burden of them. He had tried careers as an artist and a writer, and, when these seemed to founder, had been a railway clerk and a tutor, and, when even these smaller ambitions failed, he spent his final years almost bedridden, struggling with depression and dependent on alcohol and opium.

And yet he had left all around him, scattered like Sibylline leaves, the evidence of his genius: translations of Horace, powerful portraits of himself and his sisters (he later erased himself from that family group), and, of course, the inspiration he himself gave to the others, all apparently amounting to nothing, he must have thought, in those last, desperate years.

And yet it was their loving father, the Revd Patrick Brontë – hard-pressed clergyman and perpetual curate – who looked after his tragic son, and loved him as deeply as his brilliant daughters. On Easter Day – the day before my visit to the museum in Hawarth – I heard a very moving sermon in the little church in Stanbury, which Charlotte's husband had founded as a Sunday school.

'How early on that first day was the resurrection?' the preacher asked. 'We think of it as coinciding with the dawn, but we would be wrong. The women arrived "whilst it was yet dark" to find the tomb empty – the resurrection had already happened. God was most powerfully at work in the deep darkness well before the dawn. He does not wait for the light to dawn in our lives before he comes to find and raise us, but it is just when things seem most dark and hopeless for us, long before dawn, that he makes his move.'

I remembered that sermon, standing in Branwell's room, and prayed for him, and for so many others I've known like him, and for the bit of me that is like him, too – prayed that we might all find our peace in Christ and rise with him in glory.

32

A Prayer Under the New Moon

After the glorious full moon that, sailing majestically above the West Yorkshire moors, shone for our Easter, and which I watched in awe, we have come, in the first days of May, to the new moon again.

Home at last, I glimpse her silver crescent above the little town of North Walsham. There is something magical, something hopeful, in the gradually opening crescent of the new moon, the sliver of shining silver that so often glimmers in Samuel Palmer's mysterious and luminous paintings; and, when I glimpse her, especially through trees or reflected in water, I feel that something lovely, something unearthly, is about to happen.

So, I am glad that some serendipity has also brought me in my psalter to Psalm 81: 'Blow up the trumpet in the new-moon: even in the time appointed, and upon our solemn feast-day.'

After the sorrow and lamentation expressed in Psalms 79 and 80, Psalm 81 comes as a beautiful moment of uplift, with the sound of trumpets and the clear shining beauty of the new moon. Then, that psalm turns and looks back to all that God has done for Israel in the past, how he had 'eased their shoulder from the burden', and that renewed memory of grace gives the psalmist confidence for the future.

Looking up at the new moon now, after a day in which every news bulletin and every conversation seemed to turn on the darkness of the present time, the fear that the war in Ukraine, dreadful as it already is, might spread more widely, I found myself not only returning to that psalm, but also remembering how my response to it in *David's Crown* – a response written amid the fear and weariness of the first awful waves of Covid before the vaccine – also looked up towards the growing clarity of the new moon shining high above our passing troubles, as a symbol of hope, and looked back at what God has already done for us.

I wrote it then as a prayer to Christ, recalling all he achieved for us at Easter, and praying for encouragement and a sign amid our troubles. I pray it even more fervently now:

Psalm 81: Exultate Deo

Till shadows flee at last, and sorrows cease
Come down and ease our shoulders from the burden
To give our straining hearts some soft release,

Lest from sheer weariness they shrink and harden.
Refresh us with the memory of grace,
Remind us of your mercy, of that pardon

You won for us forever from the cross.
Then we will lift a lighter song to you
And glimpse beyond our loneliness and loss

The lovely new moon shining, and the true
Signs of the kingdom coming, where they gleam
And kindle in the east, still showing through

This present darkness, even as a dream
Of light before the dawn. Send us a sign
That things are not so hopeless as they seem.

33

Stevenson's Pipe

Some years ago, in these pages, I celebrated Robert Louis Stevenson's magnificent and subversive essay 'An Apology For Idlers', and reflected on how ironic it was that *Virginibus Puerisque*, the book from which it comes, was so often a set text in schools, since its chief essay is really an encomium of truantry. As Stevenson wrote, 'If you look back on your own education, I'm sure it will not be the full, vivid, instructive hours of truantry that you will regret; you would rather cancel some lacklustre periods between sleep and waking in the class.'

I recall the essay now as, in a little mild truantry of my own, I strayed into the Makar's Court, the Poet's Corner of Edinburgh, on my way to give a lecture at New College. As I had a little time to spare, I dipped into the Writers' Museum there, a fine old house full of the memorabilia of three great Scottish writers: Burns, Scott and Stevenson.

And there, in the Stevenson rooms, I came face to face with all the accoutrements of Stevenson's own ideal of truantry: his fishing rod and creel, and, best of all, his beautiful meerschaum pipe. Immediately, I could picture Stevenson, as he himself pictured his ideal truant: 'He may pitch on some tuft of lilacs over a burn and smoke innumerable pipes to the tune of the water in the stones. A bird will sing in the thicket. And there he may fall into a vein of kindly thought and see things in a new perspective.'

No truant schoolboy, though, was likely to have a pipe as beautiful as the one in the museum display case. The delicate meerschaum of the bowl has worn as smooth as porcelain, and is tinged and patterned with darker blushes of the warmth of the fragrant tobaccos it once burned; for meerschaum takes on something of their character. It has a silver band on the diamond-shaped shaft, and a beautiful amber mouthpiece.

RLS knew how to live lightly, and could make do with almost nothing – and often did, in his wanderings – but he also knew how to celebrate his little pleasures. Next to the pipe in the display case is part of an adulatory poem to that very pipe:

To My Pipe

A golden service, most loveworthy yoke.
Thou O my pipe imposest when thy bowl
Alternate dusks and quickens like a coal
At every inhalation of sweet smoke …
This service I do pay thee, thus adore
The healing power in thy soft office shed
To dull old griefs and ease harassing thought.

It's a little florid, a little over the top for modern tastes; but I love the description of how the bowl 'alternate dusks and quickens like a coal' with each draw of smoke, and I can imagine Stevenson smoking that very pipe even as he composed its poem.

I sat afterwards to smoke an idle pipe on a bench in the Makar's Court, whose stones are all inscribed with golden phrases from Scottish writers, past and present, and fell into such 'a vein of kindly thought', as Stevenson says, that I almost missed my own lecture.

34

Ranworth Rose

When we retired to Norfolk, I imagined many idyllic days on the Broads, following the counsel of Ratty in *The Wind in the Willows* and 'simply messing about in boats'. To that end, as a step up from *Willow*, the little sailing canoe that I kept on the Cam, I acquired a lovely 20-foot sailing cutter, built by a local Broadsman and happily named *Ranworth Rose*.

Her maker came from the village of Ranworth, which boasts a fine medieval church dedicated in honour of St Helen, and sometimes known as 'the cathedral of the Broads', as its tall tower can be seen from miles around and is a familiar sight to boaters. The main body of the church is fourteenth-century, although there has been a church there since Anglo-Saxon times.

But the real treasure of that church, apart from the tower, which gives you such a fine view of the Broads themselves, spread out like a map below you, is the extraordinary rood screen. Amazingly, it remains entire and intact, and the beautiful images of the angels, saints and apostles, covered for centuries by whitewash, have been uncovered and carefully restored, so that it now holds what Sir Simon Jenkins has called 'England's finest church screen paintings'.

They are so fresh and delicate, and some of them are so clear and finely detailed, that you might think that the paint was scarcely dry. The fine grey feathers on St Michael's wings contrast with the feathery gold of his armour, as he treads barefoot on the dragon with an almost nonchalant expression, a kind of musing, unconcerned contemplation.

The twelve apostles occupy the centre, of course, but St George and St Michael also have their place; and then, remarkably, the whole group is flanked by a cohort of the great female saints: St Mary Salome, with Sts John and James as toddlers; St Mary Cleophas with her four toddlers: Sts James the Less, Simon, Jude and Joseph, some of them playing with model boats and windmills – these two could compose a medieval mums-and-toddlers group just on their own; the Blessed Virgin Mary herself is there as well; and then, flanking all these, there are the formidable figures of St Etheldreda and St Barbara. When it comes to the profile of women in the church and, indeed, to being 'family-friendly', it seems that St Helen's, Ranworth, was well ahead of the curve.

But there is more; for, on the other side of the screen, covered by the choir stall misericords, they found the 'Ranworth Roses': finely stylised, five-petalled images of the white rose of the House of York, hidden for more than 450 years behind those miserere stalls, and seen again for the first time only in 1996. And it was these that first drew me to the church; for they were also painted, delicately, on the wood panels of my own *Ranworth Rose*.

I have not sailed her anything like as much as I had hoped or imagined; for retirement turns out not to be so retiring, after all. But, this year, I found her a mooring in Ranworth itself, and brought her home, as it were. So I came to Ranworth by water, as they did in the Middle Ages, and, once my boat was snug and set in her new berth, I made a pilgrimage up the lane to her mother church, said a prayer of thanksgiving for my little boat, and added a heartfelt petition that I might have a little more time to mess about in her.

35

Distant Jubilation

Looking back over my life, in my 65th year, it amazes me to think that, for as long as I have been alive and longer, our Queen has been on the throne. Amid all my ups and downs, my own crises and celebrations, my journey through the ages and stages of manhood, her reign has been a constant.

So much else has changed in those years, so much has been altered or disappeared altogether. Social trends and fashionable theories have come and gone, chasing one another's tails, the speciously up-to-date always becoming, as it must, the pathetically dated, the once cutting-edge technologies blunted and gathering dust. Whole political dynasties have risen and fallen.

And yet, among all these fleeting changes and chances, she has given us a long, faithful, deeply covenanted continuity. I rejoice in it. Her present ministers of state have scarcely been capable of seeing that we are 'godly and quietly governed', but at least we have a Queen and governor who really does know, and faithfully shows, whose minister she is.

By some miscalculation or lack of foresight, I find myself once more on the wrong side of the Atlantic as the great weekend of the Jubilee festivities arrive. I shall miss the street parties and the bunting, and, sadly, the famous trifle. I shall be in Canada, where I am sure there will be some celebration, too; but, even at a distance, I shall partake, I shall participate in heart and soul, and feel myself caught up collectively with my whole nation in a great historical moment.

I do, though, wish I could be in North Walsham for the great occasion. The June page of our kitchen calendar gives wonderful black-and-white photographs of the North Walsham market square, all strung up with flags and bunting and with long trestle tables, groaning with food, all set out for Victoria's Diamond Jubilee, and the good market townsfolk and the sturdy Norfolk farmers and tradesmen all dressed in their Sunday best for the occasion. Now, their children's children's children's children will be doing the same, in the same place.

But even the long continuity of this reign is, of course, no more than a brief moment of reflective stillness, a patch of calm water in the constant swirling and shifting falls and eddies in the stream of time, flowing away from us the moment we try to grasp it. 'Panta rhei', Heraclitus says: 'Everything flows.'

Well, not quite everything. It may be true that you cannot step into the same river twice, or even once, but there is something that 'stays amidst the things that will not stay'; there is One who is the same yesterday, today and tomorrow, from the first moment of time to the last. He is the One from whom our own sovereign's sovereignty ultimately derives, and, with him, in the moment we turn to him afresh, any and every moment can be jubilee.

36

Waiting for the Tide

Maggie and I have been away for a few days' post-Easter break in Blakeney, up on the Norfolk coast. It's a lovely place. Its narrow high street, lined with small flint-built cottages, leads down to the harbour and the quay, though to call it a harbour may give the wrong impression. When the tide is out, the sea is so far withdrawn that you don't see it at all. What you see, instead, is a narrow little channel, with only inches of water, winding its mazy way amid marshes and sandbanks, out at last towards Blakeney point, where the seals bask, and then out to the sea itself.

If you wander down to the quay at low tide, you see the mix of sturdy little double-ended fishing boats and occasional pleasure craft all wallowing in the mud, their masts dipping at odd angles, all lying higgledy-piggledy and apparently useless. But saunter down to the quay a few hours later, and there they all are, afloat and trim, bobbing eagerly at their mooring ropes or anchors, floating ever more assuredly as the incoming tide ripples past their prows. The place and its boats are transformed.

Then the quay is crowded with children fishing for crabs, and the real crab and lobster fishermen loading gear on to their boats, and tourists eagerly reading the notices about trips to see the seals, although most of these leave from Moreston nearby, where the tide has not so far to come in.

We did, of course, go out to see the seals – and, as always, as soon as our skipper untied the mooring ropes, started the kick and throb of an old diesel engine, and swayed for balance on his long tiller, I felt the sheer thrill of being afloat at last, loosed of the land's long cares and ready for adventure.

I was glad, though, to be in expert hands; for, in what seemed wide stretches of open water, there were many hidden bars and sandbanks that a receding tide would uncover – and, even out of the harbour and beyond the point itself, where we rocked up and down in small sharp waves and a keen wind, coming close to the exposed shore to see the seals, we were sailing in a place that would be dry land a few hours later.

The seals were magnificent, basking in the bright April sun and doing what all clergy should do in the week after Easter: absolutely nothing.

Back at Blakeney that evening, smoking a meditative pipe on the quayside, where all the boats were once more stuck in the mud, I found myself reflecting on the implicit wisdom of the rhythm of the tides. When the tide is out, every boatman knows that he can do nothing but wait. Rocking those grounded boats and straining to get them into some slightly deeper patch of water would achieve nothing but exhaustion. And so it is, perhaps, for all of us in our different endeavours; for, as Shakespeare observed:

There is a tide in the affairs of men
Which, taken at the flood, leads on to fortune;
Omitted, all the voyage of their life
Is bound in shallows and in miseries.

It is better to accept and live with these tides, these ups and downs, and not to blame ourselves too much when there is no water under our keel. Another tide is coming in to lift us – and, of course, Easter itself is a promise of that tide of glory which will one day lift every keel out of the sluggish muddiness of our mortality and into life in all its fullness.

37

Trinity Sunday

I have been away for the feast of the Ascension, away for the Jubilee, away for Pentecost, but I shall, at last, be home for Trinity Sunday. And, on Trinity Sunday, I can make up for lost time; for in some ways it gathers into itself all the other times and seasons: Advent, Christmas and Epiphany, bringing us the Son who reveals to us who our Father is; Holy Week and Easter, showing the full extent of his love; Pentecost, releasing the power and comfort of the Spirit – all these are involved and rolled together in the feast of the Trinity.

I rather liked it in the old dispensation when all the Sundays from then on until the next Advent were Sundays after Trinity; for even all those Sundays were not enough to fathom that mystery of the Three-in-One.

On Trinity Sunday, I notice that, quite often, incumbents shy away from preaching, and leave it to the curate or the visiting preacher. Is it modest hesitancy before the awesome mystery? Fear of falling into some obscure heresy they half-remember from church history? Dismay in the face of an incomprehensible Athanasian Creed? Whatever the reason, there's a certain reluctance to preach on this day, or to go much beyond St Patrick's approach of holding up a shamrock and hoping for the best.

I was determined, therefore, to include a poem, 'Trinity Sunday', in my sequence of sonnets for the Christian year, if only to offer all those hard-pressed curates a get-out-of-jail card: the chance to substitute a sonnet for a sermon.

Of course, George Herbert got there before me, with his lovely little poem 'Trinitie Sunday', its three verses, each of three lines, gently acknowledging the part played by the whole Trinity in his life: formed by the Father, redeemed by the Son, sanctified by the Spirit; and concluding with his own trinities – of heart, mouth and hands; faith, hope and charity; running, rising and resting with God.

Trinitie Sunday

Lord, who hast form'd me out of mud,
And hast redeem'd me through thy bloud,
And sanctifi'd me to do good;

Purge all my sinnes done heretofore:
For I confesse my heavie score,
And I will strive to sinne no more.

Enrich my heart, mouth, hands in me,
With faith, with hope, with charitie;
That I may runne, rise, rest with thee.

So, I borrowed Herbert's title, and also his little hint that the image of God in us is also Trinitarian, for my own poem:

Trinity Sunday

In the Beginning, not in time or space,
But in the quick before both space and time,
In Life, in Love, in co-inherent Grace,
In three in one and one in three, in rhyme,
In music, in the whole creation story,
In His own image, His imagination,
The Triune Poet makes us for His glory,
And makes us each the other's inspiration.
He calls us out of darkness, chaos, chance,
To improvise a music of our own,
To sing the chord that calls us to the dance,
Three notes resounding from a single tone,
To sing the End in whom we all begin;
Our God beyond, beside us, and within.

38

A Little Reminder of Liberty

The disadvantage of having had to reshelve my library on moving house is that I can never find the book I'm looking for. The advantage is that I can always find the book I'm not looking for! So it was the other day when, looking in vain for something heavy by T. S. Eliot, I happened upon something light and lovely by Richard Lovelace.

The Lovelace lyric was in a little vellum-bound volume that caught my eye as I was scanning my shelves. It bore the two words *English Lyrics* on its spine. I pulled it off the shelf, and remembered how this volume had first caught my eye 45 years earlier, when, as a student, I was browsing in a second-hand bookshop in Cambridge.

Published in 1883, it is a lovely piece of late-Victorian Aestheticism, its handmade paper beautifully set and printed, with the title page in red as well as black ink. It's a collection of lyric poems from the early sixteenth to the nineteenth centuries, from Thomas Wyatt to Thomas Lovel Beddoes; and, on that day in 1978, it was all mine for a fiver – a sum that would now scarcely buy me a pint in London!

I pulled it fondly from the shelf, remembering what pleasure it had given me, both the day I bought it – my first vellum-bound book – and over the many years since, dipping into it for its sheer variety: Herbert and Herrick were there, but so were Byron and Shelley, and often, when I discovered a new poet by randomly opening the pages of this anthology, I would then go into the college library to read and find out more. It was like being given a key, or a map, or the freedom of a literary city.

And, on this occasion, as I pulled it from the shelf, the book fell open at a few choice lyrics by Sir Richard Lovelace, and I found myself rereading, rediscovering, his famous poem 'To Althea, from Prison'. Poor Lovelace, that archetypal Royalist and Cavalier poet, had been sent by the people of Kent, his own county, to deliver a Royalist petition to Parliament, and was arrested for his pains and imprisoned in the Gatehouse Prison adjoining Westminster Abbey. Such was the response of the Mother of Parliaments to the petitions of the people.

What he chose to write in prison was a defiant poem in praise of liberty. Everyone knows the famous opening of its final verse:

Stone walls do not a prison make,
Nor iron bars a cage;
Minds innocent and quiet take
That for an hermitage.

But perhaps the lines that follow are less famous, though they beautifully summarise the whole poem. The poem moves from a celebration of his freedom in love, free to love 'Althea', wherever he is, to his freedom to honour and praise the King, even when imprisoned by the Parliament that opposed him; and so, in the very last lines, he sums those freedoms up:

If I have freedom in my love,
And in my soul am free,
Angels alone, that soar above,
Enjoy such liberty.

I was glad to have happened again upon a little book that had so enlarged and freed my mind as a young man. As I reshelved it, I found myself hoping that a book with this poem in it is still to be found somewhere in every prison library.

39

The Ancient Mariner

Two roses grow in the little bed just in front of 'The Temple of Peace', my writing hut. One is called 'The Poet's Wife' and the other 'The Ancient Mariner'. The Poet's Wife is, I am happy to say, flourishing and beautiful, but the Ancient Mariner is looking a bit bedraggled and sorry for itself, in spite of tending, feeding and pruning. It's appropriate perhaps that The Ancient Mariner should wilt a little since so much of that great poem is about being more than just bedraggled, but about being in the depth and agony of isolation. For that reason it has become something of a Covid lockdown poem. Indeed there has recently been an Internet reading of it in which all kinds of celebrities took turns, each to read a verse. I'm not so sure about the success of this project. I think the poem builds and develops precisely because it is a single voice, the voice of personal experience, telling the tale, but the celebrities were certainly right in thinking the poem has something to say to us now. Not just in the famous and perhaps obvious moments of acute loneliness:

Alone, alone, all, all alone,
Alone on a wide wide sea!
And never a saint took pity on
My soul in agony.

But much more, in the development of the story. For if the poem plots a journey into loneliness and isolation, it is a journey out and back again, and the return is a return to empathy and compassion, to a whole new vision of how to live. In slaying the albatross the Mariner demonstrated a complete lack of empathy and a failure to understand how we are all interwoven in a single web of life, but he soon learns otherwise, the hard way, as we are learning too. And one of his teachers is the terrible death-toll among his fellow travellers, and a kind of survivor guilt. As the other crew members succumb to their mysterious deaths, the Mariner suddenly sees their worth, so in the stanza that follows 'Alone, alone' he says:

> The many men, so beautiful!
> And they all dead did lie:
> And a thousand thousand slimy things
> Lived on; and so did I.

Later in the poem he comes to recognise God's beauty and joy in every living thing and even, eventually, in himself. The transition comes through a crisis and a renewal in prayer. At first he cannot pray at all, he finds his heart has become 'as dry as dust', but then under a miraculous moonrise, he finds himself blessing his fellow creatures, the many-coloured watersnakes, whom he had despised:

> The self-same moment I could pray;
> And from my neck so free
> The Albatross fell off, and sank
> Like lead into the sea.

The Mariner returns with a new sense that the life of prayer and the commandment to love are two aspects of the same thing – 'he prayeth best who loveth best', the core message he passes on to the hapless wedding guest and to the reader. It is curious that the whole poem takes place in a conversation outside, not inside, a church door. Maybe we too will have had encounters outside our churches, which will change our understanding of what goes on inside them!

40

Mysterious Ascensions

I used to find Ascension Day challenging and difficult, and this was because, at first, I tried to understand it only at a literal level. In an age that conceived the heavens, the dwelling place of 'God most high', as, in some sense, literally above us, a place in or beyond the sky, it made perfect sense, if one wanted to envisage Jesus's returning to the Father, bringing with him his humanity and ours, to the heart of heaven, to picture him literally and physically ascending in a kind of holy lift-off.

But, once we had begun to understand the solar system, let alone explore it for ourselves, the literal understanding of ascension made no sense at all. Indeed, on a spinning world, the very direction of such an ascension is changing every second.

And yet the deeper meaning of the ascension, the truth to which that old image gestures, to which it bears witness, remains as essential as ever. Heaven is not a physical location to which we can navigate in the present frame of time and space; indeed, St Augustine knew that ages ago when he said that we do not come to heaven by navigation, but by love.

Heaven is the centre of that immense mystery from which time and space themselves came into being; it is the heart of God himself, the source and centre of all, and yet transcending all creation; and the metaphor of height, of the mountain above the valley, suggests something of that transcendence.

But, by itself, unmodified by other metaphors, the metaphor of height may be misleading. Dante deals with this difficulty brilliantly when, after his long ascent up the spiral path of mount purgatory, up to the Garden of Eden, the earthly paradise, and then his glorious ascent with Beatrice up through all the spheres of the heavens, as the medieval mind imagined them, he discovers, when he gets to the highest and outermost sphere, that he has really been moving not outwards from sphere to sphere, but inwards into that centre of pure love from which the cosmos radiates like the petals of a rose.

Of course, the most important truth that Dante mediates is that Christ's ascension is our ascension, too; he takes us with him, our great high priest who has passed into the heavens. I tried to suggest a little of that in my own sonnet on the ascension in the lines:

We saw him go and yet we were not parted,
He took us with him to the heart of things,
The heart that broke for all the broken-hearted
Is whole and heaven-centred now ...

But the English mystic who really understood the ascension, and saw it in the light not just of the resurrection, but even of the cross, was Thomas Traherne. In one of his meditations on the cross, he has those astonishing lines: 'The Cross of Christ is the Jacob's ladder by which we ascend into the highest heavens ... Teach me, O Lord, these mysterious ascensions. By descending into Hell for the sake of others, let me ascend into the glory of the Highest Heavens.'

That gets to the heart of the meaning of the ascension, and that provocative plural, 'these many ascensions', makes sense of that great moment in every eucharist, the Sursum Corda: 'Lift up your hearts. *We lift them to the Lord.*'

Perhaps we can lift our hearts only in each eucharist because Christ has lifted them already – because, as St Paul says, our 'life is hidden with Christ in God'.

41

The Right Word

Like most poets, I take a delight in language and savour words for their own sake, and I take special pleasure in a rare or unusual word that happens to carry just the right meaning for the occasion on which it is used. One such word is 'susurration', meaning a whispering or murmuring sound, from the Latin root *susurrus*, a whisper, and *susurrare*, to murmur or hum.

Susurration is especially used to describe the sound that trees make when a light breeze blows through their leaves. Part of the pleasure in using it is the element of onomatopoeia; for it sounds very much like what it describes. Indeed, there was a BBC Radio 4 programme, *The Susurrations of Trees*, which celebrated that sound, in itself and in literature.

That programme noted that writers who lived before the constant wash and hum of background cars and planes heard the trees more keenly, as the delicate observations in the opening of Thomas Hardy's *Under the Greenwood Tree* testify: 'To dwellers in a wood almost every species of tree has its voice as well as its feature. At the passing of the breeze the fir-trees sob and moan no less distinctly than they rock; the holly whistles as it battles with itself; the ash hisses amid its quiverings; the beech rustles while its flat boughs rise and fall.'

The same programme spoke of 'the distinctive susurrations of several species: quivering poplars, aspens that sound like rain, rattling London planes, whispering elms, the hiss of the ash, whooshing pines and the strangely silent yew'.

I have not yet had the opportunity to use susurration in a poem, but the day is coming.

On the other hand, I also delight in plain language, in the distinct and pungent accuracy of words of one syllable; and I particularly appreciate it in street and place names, the ones real people have used from time immemorial rather than the ones recently invented and imposed by town planners. There is something satisfying about Main Street and High Street. You know what it is, and you know where you are. Better still, in some small Norfolk villages, your address will simply be 1 The Street; there is only one street, and you are on it.

Likewise, almost every village on the Broads has a Staithe Road, which, quite properly and without diversion, leads down to the staithe. Staithe is itself a wonderful word, a survival into Middle and then modern English of the Old English word *stæþ*, meaning a wooden landing stage, itself derived from the Old Norse *stöð*, which meant harbour. There, in the one simple word, is a little history of East Anglia, taking us back to the Vikings – and the Vikings, I note, is the name of the North Walsham Rugby team; perhaps the team includes some descendant of the intrepid Norsemen who first found a *stöð* in Norfolk.

I sometimes wonder whether theologians, too, might benefit from attention to plain language, as well as to Greek or Latinate abstractions; and perhaps when they have written 'We affirm the eschatological dimension of the *kerygma*' they might more plainly say, 'We speak of the hope that is in us.' Karl Barth, I believe, did this; for there is a story that he was once asked in a radio interview whether he could sum up the whole of his multi-volume *Church Dogmatics* in brief words for the layman. 'Yes,' he said, 'it really amounts to this: Jesus loves me, this I know, For the Bible tells me so.'

42

Pentecost and Translation

Some years ago, as we came to the 400th anniversary of the Authorised Version of the Bible, I was asked to give a paper on Lancelot Andrewes, who had headed the First Westminster Company of translators and done much of the translation work himself. I wanted to find out whether he had, in any sense, a 'theology of translation'. So, I read the complete run of his Pentecost sermons from 1604, when the work was commissioned, to 1611, when it was completed; and a wonderful and distinctly Pentecostal theology of translation did, indeed, emerge.

At the core of it was a delight in language itself, and the sheer diversity and variety of languages. It was a patristic commonplace to say that the miracle of translation at Pentecost was, in some sense, an undoing or reversal of the 'confusion of tongues' at Babel. But, Andrewes points out, Pentecost is not strictly a *reversal* of Babel. If that were so, then all those people of diverse languages who heard the apostles would have suddenly understood Hebrew, and we would be back to Babel's uniformity.

The Tower of Babel presents us with an image of arrogant human power: monoglot, mono-cultural, a triumphalist technology stamping its uniform logo on everything. God's response, according to Andrewes, is not only to break the tower, but also to break the linguistic monopoly, and to scatter abroad into the world thousands of unique languages, each with its own way of imagining and describing the world. While the 'curse' of Babel leads to 'confusion of tongues', it is also a blessing that leads to rich diversity and breadth of perspective.

And so, Andrewes says, God blesses the multiplicity of tongues and graces of every language with his gospel, because the sending of the Holy Spirit was 'a benefit so great and so wonderful as there were not tongues enough on earth to celebrate it'.

As he goes on to say: 'And so, by speaking all tongues they have gathered a church that speaks all tongues; a thing much tending to the glory of God. And indeed it was not meet one tongue only should be employed that way … but that all tongues should do it; which as a concert of many instruments might yield a full harmony. In which we behold the mighty work of God, that the same means of several tongues, which was the destroying of Babel, the very same is here made to work the building of Zion …'

In the sermons, Andrewes raises the obvious questions about the dangers of mistranslation and misunderstanding. Might not God be afraid of his Word being misinterpreted, or lost in translation?

Not at all, Andrewes says; for God himself has already made, and risked, the greatest translation of all, when the Word was made flesh. Indeed, in one of his sublime Christmas sermons, he takes a translation of Hebrew to make that very point: 'The word that is Hebrew for flesh the same is also Hebrew for good tidings – as we call it, the Gospel, sure not without the Holy Ghost so dispensing it, there could be no other meaning but that some incarnation, or making flesh, should be generally good news for the whole world. To let us know this good tidings is come to pass he tells us the Word is now become flesh.'

Those insights of Andrewes's certainly contributed to the closing couplet of my own sonnet on Pentecost: 'Today the lost are found in his translation, Whose mother-tongue is Love, in every nation.'

43

The Kingfisher and the Heron

With the gradual easing of the Covid lockdown I have managed to get away from my usual haunts and spend most of the day in a little boat on the Norfolk Broads. Amid the quiet delights of that watery world I was rewarded with two beautiful sights: the darting of a kingfisher in the morning, and in the evening, first a glimpse of a slow grey heron rising and falling ahead of me, and, as I turned in by some trees to berth the boat, a much closer glimpse of the heron itself: still, stately, perched patiently on a branch, watching the river as it flowed past carrying me and my little boat back to our mooring.

There was a great deal to savour in the contrast between these two extraordinary birds. In the grey and rainy morning the sudden sweet darting of bright blue, reflected in the river, just under the shelter of low branches was like a flash of hidden colour into a monochrome world, indeed almost like a vision from another world, as though a sliver of blue sky from Shakespeare's 'eternal summer' had shimmered a moment into our dark time and disappeared again, leaving behind a little thrill of hope. I never see kingfishers when I'm looking for them, they just appear magically and disappear as quickly, an unexpected grace that never fails to make my day.

The quiet evening was as grey as the morning had been, but the rain had given way first to mist and then a gentle breeze when my homeward-guiding heron appeared. It is extraordinary that we can use the same word 'bird', and recognise what is common, between two such different and contrastingly beautiful creatures. But the slow, lazy flapping, the long low dipping glides, and then the final stillness of the heron, all suited and expressed my evening and homing mood, just as much as the kingfisher's blue bolt had electrified and alerted my morning.

I learned from Coleridge not only to love birds in and for themselves, as God's good creatures whom he also loves, as he loves us, but also to recognise that these creatures, breathed into being by God as he forms and sustains all things, are also part of both God's mind and ours. They are creatures in their own right but they are also forms of thought, and, like all of nature, they provide us with the images and emblems with which we think, 'lovely shapes and sounds intelligible of the eternal language' which God utters in and through us, even as he gives us both life.

So, in one sense I recognised something of myself in both the kingfisher and the heron. At first, perhaps prompted by the contrast of morning and evening, I thought of the kingfisher as my younger self: bright, energetic, making swift, sudden, unpredictable darts and flights, and I wondered if the slow patience of the evening heron, perched like a grey hermit in contemplation of the river might be an emblem of 'the gifts reserved for age'. But I'm not sure that's quite right. I think there is always, in all of us, something of both the kingfisher and the heron, the morning and the evening. Perhaps our best emblem is the river itself. We float in the little boat of our consciousness on the surface of something deep and mysterious, always arising freshly from its source, and if we are patient and attentive, both the kingfishers and the herons of the mind will come and bless us.

44

Returning to Ely

I returned recently to my old haunts in Ely. I never cease to be astonished by the cathedral, which you see from miles away, almost floating above the surrounding fenland, well deserving her nickname 'the ship of the fens'. She seems to draw you towards her; yet, she does not dominate so much as grace the little city above which she rises.

Returning to Ely now, I call to mind the day I was ordained there, 33 years ago, and then my time as a curate at St Mary's, and, after that, while serving in the diocese, my various returns to the 'mother church'.

One such return was especially memorable. I was a team vicar in Huntingdon, and I decided to bring our youth group on a canoeing pilgrimage to the shrine of Etheldreda in the great cathedral. I thought that it would be interesting to make the journey entirely by water, as must have been done when the Isle of Ely was really an isle.

To give our pilgrimage some focus, the youth of the parish visited older parishioners, and asked them each to write down a prayer, which we would gather together and take to the shrine. We managed to beg and borrow enough canoes, and coax a parishioner to accompany us in their motor cruiser, as safety ship and provider of food and rest. We made our way, over several days, along the great Ouse, bearing our box of prayers.

When we arrived, at last, one of the canons came down to greet us, and we made our way in procession, up Fore Hill, and into the cathedral, entering, as I did at my ordination, through the little door set in the great west door, amazed, as I had been then, that such a small entrance could lead into such numinous immensity.

After our prayers had been said, we were taken, as a treat, right up into the roof space around the great octagonal lantern, and we gazed back on the winding waterways of our journey. Down there on the river, amid its twists and turns, and its high banks, our way had seemed an endless maze; but, up here, we could look back and see it all laid out in a beautifully patterned map. I hoped that that shift in perspective might give our youth an emblem with which to think about the journey of their lives; it certainly did for me.

At Etheldreda's shrine, we told again her adventurous story, her escapes from dynastic marriage, her persistent quest for the freedom to pray and to dedicate her life to Christ, her true love. That story still inspires, and just recently I wrote this sonnet for Etheldreda (with a brief nod to Elizabeth Warren in the epigraph):

St Etheldreda

'Nevertheless she persisted …'

Abbess and Princess, lend us all your strength,
Your fierce determination to be free;
Free of those cold conventions which at length
Had tethered you as married property.
Still you persisted, you would not be held
From your first love for Jesus Christ your Lord
And from that free devotion which you held,
As bride of Christ, to dwell within the Word
And let Him dwell in you as mystery:
A secret place to bide and to abide.
You slipped away to Ely with the tide;
Your Pilgrim staff became a flowering tree,
Inviting men and women equally,
To keep a soul-space open, welcome, free.

45

Remembering Shelley

I write this on the 200th anniversary of Shelley's death: an anniversary that has prompted in me many memories and grateful reflections of all that his verse has meant to me over the years.

Shelley first burst into my life when, as an ardent, romantic and poetry-loving teenager, I 'discovered' him and fell in love not only with his poetry, but also with his whole persona, as I understood it then: the free spirit, borne before the wind, uttering poems of lyric beauty as though they were entirely spontaneous compositions, given and inspired, the 'profuse strains of unpremeditated art', which he attributed to his skylark. He was the Shelley of André Maurois's *Ariel*, the human embodiment of the spirit Ariel in *The Tempest*, a creature of air and fire, scarcely touching the earth, until, in his tragic death at sea, he himself 'suffered a sea-change into something rich and strange'.

Then, as I matured a little, and turned my attention through and beyond poetry to history and politics, it was the radical Shelley, the Shelley of *Queen Mab* and *The Masque of Anarchy* who became my guiding spirit: Shelley the champion of radical freedom in the face of political oppression; the Shelley who could switch from a highly wrought Platonic ode to the rousing song of a revolutionary ballad, and call on the oppressed to

Rise like Lions after slumber
In unvanquishable number –
Shake your chains to earth like dew
Which in sleep had fallen on you –
Ye are many – they are few.

Later still, as I enjoyed and endured the raptures, but also the complexities and ambiguities, of love and loving, the Shelley who moved me was the poet of the divided and yet still exuberant heart – the poet who expressed so perfectly that ardent longing for the unattainable which is at the heart of all our desire:

The desire of the moth for the star,
Of the night for the morrow,
The devotion to something afar
From the sphere of our sorrow.

And, when I came to faith, the faith that Shelley had specifically rejected in his early pamphlet *The Necessity of Atheism*, I found, surprisingly, as C. S. Lewis also did, that Shelley was still at my side, still speaking to and for my heart; for he, too, had intuited that, somewhere in all our earthly loves and longings, there is a desire for the heavenly; there is a 'worship the heart lifts above, And the Heavens reject not'.

And now I find that 'Ode to the West Wind', perhaps his greatest poem, which my mother used to recite to me as a child, and which I used to shout to the winds myself with all the ardour and abandon of my teenage years, still stirs me in my sixties. But now it has given me words not only to address the west wind, but the words of a prayer to the Holy Spirit: not merely 'the breath of Autumn's being', but the breath, the energy, the inspiration of my loving and redeeming God:

Make me thy lyre, even as the forest is:
What if my leaves are falling like its own!
… Be thou, Spirit fierce,
My spirit! Be thou me, impetuous one!
Drive my dead thoughts over the universe
Like wither'd leaves to quicken a new birth!

46

A Choice of Signs

Deep in the Undercroft Museum at York Minster there's a little clay tile which is, for me, almost as moving as the entire minster that contains it. For inscribed discretely, perhaps hastily, on that tile, dating from around AD 100 is the chi-rho, the two Greek letters that stand for Christ and are the mark of a Christian. Earlier than the earliest church, earlier than the creeds, as early perhaps as the Gospels themselves, here is the evidence of the good news of Christ's resurrection reaching England, before it was England. Somebody, perhaps a slave, perhaps an adjunct or auxiliary of the Roman Army's fortifications at Eboracum, had carried the faith, even as far as this *ultima Thule*, this furthest flung outpost of empire, and chosen, for a moment, to leave the mark of their faith on a clay tile before it dried.

The tall minster that towers above that little tile bears witness to the eventual ascendence of the Christian faith, and to its persistence, its capacity, time and again, after every defeat, to recover and rise again from the ashes, as indeed the minster itself has done, seven times burned and seven times rebuilt, as I remembered in a poem addressed to the minster in my collection *The Singing Bowl*:

> York Minster broken bone-house, broken home
> Of broken bread, in all your funeral rites
> You witness Resurrection. Seven times
> Your skeleton has crumbled into ash …
> Stand up old stones, hold in your bones the light,
> The dispensation to each piling year
> Of Love's abiding truth.

But the minster itself, in all its splendour, makes a more

ambiguous witness too, a witness to the church's gradual accumulation of wealth, and power and privilege, a development which could scarcely be imagined by the un-named underling who dared to inscribe the sign of a proscribed religion on that clay tile in the undercroft. And just outside the minster of course is a modern statue of Constantine who was in York when the news reached him that he had become emperor. Legend has it that he too saw, inscribed, the chi-rho, the sign of Christ, not on a poor clay tile, but resplendent across the heavens, and heard the words *In hoc signo vinces*, by this sign conquer. So Constantine, not yet himself a Christian, had the eagles on his standards changed to the new symbol and went on, through slaughter and violence at the battle of Milvian bridge, to triumph and power as emperor.

Christians can of course be grateful to Constantine for the freedom to worship openly which was given to them in the Edict of Milan in 313, the year after that battle. But it was a tragically short step from being tolerated by the empire to using the levers of imperial power to enforce its own intolerance. Within a couple of generations, the persecuted Church was itself a persecutor.

Perhaps Constantine misunderstood his own vision. Perhaps *In hoc signo vinces* didn't mean swap emblems, exchange one logo for another. Perhaps it really meant only through Christ, and through the way of the cross, will you conquer. Only when you love your enemies and bless those who persecute you, only when you meet your adversaries with the words 'Father forgive', will Christ, who is Love, conquer through you.

The Church is once again feeling marginalised, despised and in places oppressed, but it might be better for us to take as our insignium the faithful little sign in clay below the minster's impressive edifice, rather than the statue of Constantine, at ease and in power, which stands enticingly beside it.

47

Hide and Seek

I love the old feast of Corpus Christi, or the Day of Thanksgiving for Holy Communion, as *Common Worship* calls it. My sense of its mystery came before I even began to know that it was a mystery in which I might partake. I first encountered the two words 'Corpus Christi' in the medieval Corpus Christi Carol, which I found in the anthology *Mediaeval English Lyrics*, even before I heard the setting by Benjamin Britten, or the version by the late American singer Jeff Buckley, which made it more famous and accessible.

What I loved about that mysterious lyric was the way in which the poetry, in a falcon's flight, took you through one layer of image and meaning after another, with a sense of unwrapping or penetrating a deep hiddenness: first, the 'orchard brown', and then, within the orchard, the hall, and then, in the hall, a bed, curtained with 'gold so red', and, in the bed, the wounded knight, and, by the bed, the weeping maid, then that final verse: 'And by that bed's side there stands a stone, "Corpus Christi" written thereon …'

It's as well they weren't obliged in the fourteenth century to write: 'By that bedside there stands a stone, "Day of Thanksgiving for Holy Communion" written thereon.'

There are many theories, of course, about what is going on in this carol, and how it relates both to the Arthurian myths and to the mystery of the eucharist. I find Eamon Duffy persuasive when he writes that 'there can be no question whatever' that the carol's 'strange cluster of images' are derived 'directly from the cult of the Easter Sepulchre, with its Crucifix, Host, and embroidered hangings, and the watchers kneeling around it day and night'.

But one needn't be so specific. For me, it is the inter-layering, the hiddenness, that speaks to my experience. The image of the bleeding knight, perhaps Malory's Fisher King, speaks of the Passion; and yet the use of the present continuous rather than the past tense speaks of resurrection and the eucharistic presence.

Using a very different linguistic register, I tried to get some sense of the seeking and finding, the hiding and being discovered, that happens at every communion, in my poem 'Hide and Seek':

Hide and Seek

Ready or not, you tell me, *here I come!*
And so I know I'm hiding, and I know
My hiding-place is useless. You will come
And find me. You are searching high and low.
Today I'm hiding low, down here, below,
Below the sunlit surface others see.
Oh find me quickly, quickly come to me.
And here you come and here I come to you.
I come to you because you come to me.
You know my hiding places. I know you,
I reach you through your hiding-places too;
Feeling for the thread, but now I see –
Even in darkness I can see you shine,
Risen in bread, and revelling in wine.

48

Poetry as a Way of Knowing

I am back from giving some talks and poetry readings in the States, and very glad to be home. I enjoyed some of the contrasts of that enormous country while I was there. I started in Southern California, which was, contrary to the stereotype, considerably cloudier and cooler than the England that I had left, as Californians were experiencing what they call their 'June Gloom', when a combination of sea-fret – low cloud and mist coming down from the mountains – cools and suffuses, with a kind of sepia tint, the golden sands and blue seas for which their state is famous.

There were, of course, still the palm trees and the Spanish Colonial architecture to admire; and there was the wealth and glamour by which to be intimidated. I always felt that we were driving either in or out of the album cover of the Eagles' *Hotel California*; fortunately, I was able not only to check out, but also to leave. After that, I was in Wisconsin, which was much hotter and brighter than California, and staying again at Nashotah House, a version of St Stephen's House transplanted to the Midwest, but with the addition of visiting fallow deer, chipmunks and sand cranes.

But I am happy to be home, and it feels as though, after a cold wet spring, summer has suddenly come in, in all her blossom and beauty.

I had been in the US to give some talks about how poetry is more than just a particular art form, but is also a way of knowing. I was developing Shakespeare's insight that the imagination 'apprehends more than cool reason ever comprehends', and commending Coleridge's assertion that poetry can 'remove the film of familiarity' and 'awaken the mind's attention to the loveliness and wonders before it, but for which, in consequence of that film of familiarity and self-ish solicitude we have eyes that see not, ears that hear not, and hearts that neither feel nor understand'.

My claim, in those talks, was that, once we have read and inwardly absorbed certain kinds of poetry, our perceptions are heightened and clarified. If you have Psalm 19 within you, and know that 'The heavens declare the glory of the Lord and the firmament showeth forth his handiwork', you will never see the night sky in quite the same way again.

But, once I was back home, amid the woods and fields of England, it was not the Hebrew psalmist but John Clare, that most deeply native English poet, who helped me to apprehend more, to see and to appreciate the English summer afresh, and to sense those 'intimations of immortality' to which even the most passing and changing aspects of nature seem to bear witness.

As I was enjoying all of summer's sights and scents, it was these words of Clare's which came to me, unbidden, and cleansed the doors of perception, so that I could see anew what he wonderfully calls 'the green life of change':

All nature has a feeling: woods, fields, brooks
Are life eternal; and in silence they
Speak happiness beyond the reach of books;
There's nothing mortal in them; their decay
Is the green life of change; to pass away
And come again in blooms revivified.
Its birth was heaven, eternal is its stay,
And with the sun and moon shall still abide
Beneath their day and night and heaven wide.

49

A Wake-Up Call

I was reflecting last week on the pleasure of retreating on a hot day to cooling streams, reflecting on time itself as a stream on which we might float, reflecting on the simple pleasure of 'messing about in boats'. But, even as I drifted away and left 'the false clocks with their little steps' behind, England was burning. The record-breaking heat had led to destructive fires not only in London, but all around the country, several of them in Norfolk.

Watching the news that evening, it was as though those distant but devastating Australian fires that we watched in horror at the beginning of 2020 – and then promptly forgot about, because the pandemic was upon us – had returned, but this time so much closer to home. At least we are not distracted now, and at last our attention is focused on extreme weather events that can be described only as a wake-up call.

It was in 2019, before either plague or fire had come so close to us, that I was asked by the brilliant young composer Rhiannon Randle to write a poem that she might set as an anthem for an eco-themed evensong (Choral Eco-Song, I think they called it). We both felt that the church needed prayerfully to address the crisis of climate change, and to express those concerns in her liturgy.

Notwithstanding the special theme, we were still following the standard lectionary, but how prescient and telling the lectionary readings for that particular evensong proved to be! For they both enjoined us to wake up: we had God's call to us through Isaiah: 'Rouse yourself, rouse yourself!' (Isaiah 51.17) and Jesus's words to the disciples in Gethsemane: 'Keep awake and pray' (Mark 14.38). Together, they seemed to me to form a divine wake-up call.

What emerged as I began writing was not a discursive poem, or a moral admonition, but a long cry of the earth herself – a direct appeal to us from nature, which Rhiannon set powerfully as a choir anthem. The anthem was sung at St Michael's, Cornhill, in February of 2020, when wildfires were only in distant countries, and 40°C was unthinkable in England.

I call it to mind again now – not to add to choruses of doom, but, on the contrary, because, when I revisited the poem, I found that, although it voices a great lament, it actually ends with a real hope: a hope that our Emmanuel, our God with us, will join his voice to the voice of the earth, will move by his Spirit to rouse us, even so late in the day, to repentance and to change for good:

Our Burning World

Our burning world is turning in despair,
I hear her seething, sighing through the air:
'Oh, rouse yourself, this is your wake-up call
For your pollution forms my funeral pall.
My last ice lapses, slips into the sea,
Will you unfreeze your tears and weep with me?
Or are you sleeping still, taking your rest?
The hour has come, that puts you to the test,
Wake up to change at last, and change for good,
Repent, return, re-plant the sacred wood.
You are my children, I too am God's child,
And we have both together been defiled,
But God hangs with us, on the hallowed tree
That we might both be rescued, both be free.'

50

From a Celtic Roundhouse

I am writing this from Aberdaron in the beautiful Llyn pen-
insula, where I have come to take part in the annual R. S.
Thomas and M. E. Eldridge Poetry and Arts Festival. I led
some poetry workshops, culminating in a reading of what
had been written that day. The watchword I had given my
group for the day was: 'Begin the song exactly where you
are.' We were to write with a rooted, particular, incarnate
sense of place.

We couldn't have chosen a better place in which to begin
that endeavour, for our first session took place in Sarn Plas,
the tiny white cottage to which R. S. Thomas retired when
he ceased to be Vicar of St Hywyn's, Aberdaron. It is a low
white cottage nestled into the hillside, overlooking a bay and
with glorious mountain views beyond, the views of which R.
S. Thomas wrote:

> In Wales there are jewels
> To gather, but with the eye
> Only. A hill lights up
> Suddenly; a field trembles
> With colour and goes out
> In its turn; in one day
> You can witness the extent
> Of the spectrum and grow rich
> With looking.

We did 'grow rich with looking', and some, at least, of those
riches found their way into writing.

But, if the start of our day was in one of the jewels of
Wales, our evening reading was in another; for we gathered

in the Celtic Roundhouse in Felin Uchaf. It is an extraordinary place. Built up over the past eighteen years, it describes itself as a 'cultural and eco-centre', a cluster of buildings of wood and turf and thatch, not a straight line or a hard angle in sight, but all rounded and curved, all interior beams carved and garlanded with inscriptions of poetry, everything naturally bedded in and arising from the landscape in which it is set.

Parts of it would certainly give you a sense of a Celtic settlement in the sixth century, but it also felt like a wonderful cross between Hobbiton and Lothlórien. The roundhouse in which we read seemed and, indeed, was bigger on the inside than the outside; for, from without, you saw the conical thatched roof rising from surrounding greenery, which covered some of its walls, as though the house were growing out of the greenery itself; but, inside, its walls and floor had been dug out more widely from the slight slope in which it nestled.

There was a central fire pit beneath the cone of the thatch, and benches were set in widening circles from around that centre. It was like the *ban-hus* that Heaney celebrates in his poem 'Bone Dreams':

In the coffered
riches of grammar
and declensions
I found *ban-hus*,
its fire, benches,
wattle and rafters,
where the soul
fluttered a while
in the roofspace.

Heaney deftly alludes in that poem to the passage in Bede in which a sparrow flits for a moment through the roofspace of just such a hall, and is likened to our own soul. Astonishingly, during our recitations, a swallow did just that, flitting in under the thatch eaves at one end of the roundhouse, enchanting us for a moment, and flying out through the other. There couldn't have been a better place to recite poetry.

51

Do Different

There is an old dialect saying in these parts: 'In Norfolk we do different.' This eventually became the motto of the University of East Anglia, modernised and shortened as simply, 'Do Different.'

I have certainly noticed that my newly adopted county is imbued with a robustly contrarian spirit. Unsurprisingly, Norfolk has a long history of radicalism – and, occasionally, rebellion. One has only to think of how Julian of Norwich resisted the wrathful theologies of her day with a radical new theology of Love; to think of the reforming zeal of the Lollards; or of the Peasants' Revolt, whose final battle was fought here in North Walsham; or, later still, of Kett's Rebellion.

So it didn't surprise me to discover that Tom Paine, that friend of the poor, thorn in the flesh of tyrants, and inspirer of American independence, was a Norfolk lad, born in Thetford.

I found this out when I went with Maggie to the Maids Head Hotel, a Norwich inn that goes back to the thirteenth century, to hear Rob Knee, a local historian, give an oration in the person of Paine himself, clad in eighteenth-century clothes, telling the story of his life and quoting from his works. It was a riveting tale: from his days as an apprentice staymaker in Norfolk, to his life as a customs and excise man in Lewes, to his sojourns in America and France, and then back to America, assisting in both revolutions and becoming friends with figures as diverse as William Blake and Thomas Jefferson.

But it was the readings from Paine's pamphlets that really struck home; for so many of his ideas, radical and almost unthinkable at the time, are, to quote one of his own titles, *Common Sense* now: progressive taxation to provide welfare for the poorest; free and universal education; the power, invested in ordinary people, to change their government by democratic mandate.

Even among the radical circles in which he moved, some of his ideas were too much of a challenge. His early opposition to slavery, and call for the emancipation of slaves in America, lost him much of his support there; for his friends Jefferson and Washington were both slave-owners. Some of his ideas have yet to catch on, such as his plea for a universal basic income funded by taxes on inherited wealth; and some of his opinions, especially on religion, remain as controversial as ever. He began as a Quaker and was thus already a dissenter, but, under the influence of Voltaire and others, he passed on from those radically Christian roots into the philosophical deism which characterised, for him, in the title of another of his pamphlets, *The Age of Reason*.

And here, of course, I differ from him, and place my trust not in some supreme, and supremely detached, watchmaker, but in the living and loving God I meet in Christ: one who knows what it is to be crucified as well as to be raised in glory. But, doubtless, Paine, for all that he mocks my religion, would, as a good Norfolk man, applaud my choice to 'do different' and to disagree with both his strictures and the aggressive secularism of my own age.

Certainly, the local historian who brought Paine so vividly to life that morning in Norwich also enjoyed his Norfolk freedom to 'do different'; for there he was the next Sunday, worshipping Christ with me, in our parish church. Would Paine be turning in his grave or applauding from the rafters? Perhaps both.

106

52

In Southwell Minster

I visited Southwell Minster recently to give a lecture on C. S. Lewis. Before I spoke, I had a chance to revisit the Minster's remarkable Chapter House, one of my favourite places in England. All the columns blossom into the most beautiful stone foliage, as though the stone were turning into trees, or trees had just that moment become stone; and, above these, are carved some of the most wild and enchanting 'foliate heads', or Green Men, as they came to be called by Lady Raglan in an article in *The Folklore Journal* in 1939, a name that has stuck.

I do not think that they are in the least out of place in a church or cathedral. On the contrary, they seem to me to represent, in almost human form, the wild energy, fecundity and green life of nature, the rich ecology of which Christ is also Lord. In some way, whatever their origins, they speak of the One who is life itself, and whose resurrection is the fulfilment and meaning of the rising in spring of every buried seed.

Christ does not come to destroy the old pagan pieties, but to purify and perfect them, to reveal their meaning. If he says 'a greater than Solomon is here', it is also true that, in Christ, a greater than Pan, and a greater than Dionysus, is also revealed.

When I sing my song 'The Green Man' in pubs, some of my Christian friends are puzzled or upset; but the ordinary, 'unchurched' folk at the bar are the first to see the connections, and to ask, 'Those lines where you sing "I'm the goodness in the bread, I'm the wildness in the wine", are they about communion? When you sing "If you cut me down I'll spring back green again", is that about Easter?'

Lewis certainly understood that some of those earlier pagan pieties could be brought to Christ, for the goodness and life that they celebrate belong to him. This is very clear in the scene in *Prince Caspian* when, as part of the liberation of Old Narnia from the oppression of the Telmarines, Aslan summons Dionysus, although Lewis does not give him that name, but, rather, delights to tell us his many other names: 'He seemed to have many names – Bromios, Bassareus, and the Ram were three of them. There were lots of girls with him, as wild as he.'

Then comes the great romp, the release of joy and energy which is part of liberation from any oppressive regime, and Lucy and Susan recognise their new companions with yet another name. Lucy whispers: 'I say, Sue, I know who they are.' 'Who?' 'The boy with the wild face is Bacchus and the old one on the donkey is Silenus.'

Then, in a nice touch (and not without theological significance), Susan says: 'I wouldn't have felt quite safe with Bacchus and all his wild girls if we'd met them without Aslan.' 'I should think not,' said Lucy.

The American film, I noticed, omitted this entire episode, as though the US were still locked in Prohibition; but, if we are to reach the many people, such as those who gathered at Stonehenge for the summer solstice, for whom the old pagan reverence is attractive, but the Church seems cold and distant, then we would do well to recover some of the lost language and theology that is there in the foliate faces at Southwell, and kindled for us, also, in the imagination of C. S. Lewis.

53

Under the Mercy

I had a curious experience in a graveyard last week. I was in Oxford for a week, speaking at a conference devoted to celebrating, and continuing, the work of the Oxford Inklings, whose key members were C. S. Lewis, J. R. R. Tolkien, Charles Williams and Owen Barfield. On my way to the University Church to preach a sermon at the conference's closing service, I thought that I would visit the churchyard of Holy Cross, and pay my respects to Charles Williams, who is buried there.

Williams, sometimes known as 'the oddest Inkling', was an extraordinary man: a devout Anglican, but also an adept, along with his friend Yeats, in the quasi-magical Order of the Golden Dawn. T. S. Eliot, who saw to it that Faber published his novels, thought him the holiest man he had ever met, and described the novels as 'supernatural thrillers'. Lewis was also deeply moved by his writings and his friendship, and was devastated by Williams's sudden death in 1945.

The churchyard of Holy Cross is wonderfully wild and overgrown, a haven for wild flowers, bees and insects. Not many people seem to visit it, and, wandering on the paths there, which are so tangled with long grass and nettles, I wondered whether I could find his gravestone, for the paths seemed to wind in ways that I couldn't remember. The place was quiet, deserted, and still. Just as I began to feel that I might never find the spot, there was a movement at my feet, and a beautiful black cat appeared, purring and rubbing itself round my legs; then it turned and walked away. I followed, and it led me straight to Williams's grave, where it perched on a stone and asked for more fuss as its reward, purring all the time.

It was all a little uncanny, and I felt rather as though I were in the opening scene of one of Williams's novels; for, unlike his friends Lewis and Tolkien, he did not set his books in imaginary worlds, but firmly in our own, and it is into this familiar world that the magical powers, the supernatural and spiritual presences, come unbidden. When I had given the cat its due, I turned to contemplate Williams's headstone, beautifully lettered and simple: 'Charles Walter Stansby Williams: Poet', and then, beneath the word Poet, the words with which he used to sign off all his letters: 'Under The Mercy'.

I thanked God for him and for the gift of his writings, and especially for the beautiful word 'coinherence', which he applied not just to the persons of the Trinity, as earlier theologians had done, but also to our relations with one another in Christ – and, indeed, to our relations with all the natural world; for we are all, as God's creatures, mutually interwoven, mutually interdependent, bearing one another's burdens.

I left the churchyard and went to preach my sermon in the pulpit from which Lewis had preached his wonderful sermon 'The Weight of Glory'. At the reception afterwards, I mentioned to the composer J. A. C. Redford, with whom I had collaborated on the work 'Ordinary Saints', that I had visited Williams's grave. Before I could tell him anything more, he said: 'You know, years ago I had a strange, almost a mystical, experience there. I somehow got lost in the tangled paths and couldn't find the grave, and then, from out of the undergrowth, there stepped a beautiful red fox, which looked at me, turned around, and trotted down the path that led me straight to Williams's grave.'

I told him my story, and we were silent for a while, but glad to be reminded that we, too, were 'under the mercy'.

54

Remembering Larkin

This year, the centenary of his birth, has been a time to celebrate Philip Larkin – or, at least, to celebrate and remember
his poetry, since, for many, if not most, there is much to
regret about the life and opinions of the man himself. For
me, it is the poetry that remains and, indeed, grows in
stature as the years pass; I leave judgement of the man to
others.

Larkin is the poet who restored my faith and rekindled my
interest in 'modern' poetry. Having come to poetry through
Keats and Shelley, I was attracted as much by the sound, the
music, the cadence of a singing line of verse as by its diction,
its reach, its meaning. When I read many of the poets who
were being published in the 1970s, my formative years, that
music seemed to have vanished – with lucidity, coherence,
or any other concession to the bewildered reader. And then
I discovered Larkin.

I bought *High Windows* as a 16-year-old in the year that it
came out, and then worked my way back through the three
preceding slim volumes of his poetry. And, at first, it was the
elegance of his verse, the quiet understated rhyme schemes
and rhythmic patterns, that attracted me. Here was a poet
who could use traditional metre and rhyme and yet retain
a completely contemporary voice, never distorting word
order for the sake of rhyme and metre. His deft craftsmanship never draws attention to itself, but simply undergirds
and supports the poem, like the unseen push and response
of a sprung dance floor.

It was all there in 'To the Sea', the first poem of that first
book I bought: the classic cadence, and yet the completely
contemporary voice, and that eye for ordinary prosaic

details that are, nevertheless, lifted into poetry by the understated music of the verse:

> To step over the low wall that divides
> Road from concrete walk above the shore
> Brings sharply back something known long before –
> The miniature gaiety of seasides.

It is a good poem to remember in 'idle August'; for I, too,
can wander down to the beach at Mundesley and see and
hear it all again, just as he did, but with my sight and hearing
focused by his wonderful lines:

> Steep beach, blue water, towels, red bathing caps,
> The small hushed waves' repeated fresh collapse
> Up the warm yellow sand …

And when I think to myself, 'How wonderful that it's all still
going on, just as Larkin described it 50 years ago!', I realise,
with a little shock of recognition, that I am still in Larkin's
poem; for that is just what he felt and said: 'Still going on, all
of it, still going on!'

These yearly trips to the sea have become, in Larkin's
words, 'half an annual pleasure, half a rite'. Indeed, by the
end of the poem, Larkin, so shy of religion, has discerned
something more going on in this pilgrimage to the sea, this
sharing between the generations. He famously wrote: 'If I
were called in To construct a religion I should make use of
water,' and perhaps there is something of an unacknowledged religious rite, in those final lines of 'To the Sea':

> It may be that through habit these do best,
> Coming to the water clumsily undressed
> Yearly; teaching their children by a sort
> Of clowning; helping the old, too, as they ought.

55

Moonlight and Sacrament

Like many folk who've been kept awake a little later than is their wont by these warm nights, I have been drawn by the light and beauty of the moon, and especially the 'super moon' that we had recently. Sleepless, I walked out into the balmy night, and there she was – closer it seemed, and closer indeed, to the earth. Her silver seemed somehow warmed with a golden tinge, as if more of the sun's gold itself were held and reflected from her, and she was brighter than I had known, brighter than the few streetlights that sought to rival her.

Gazing on that moon inevitably called to mind the other times when I have stood looking at her, and also gave me a kind of fellowship with all who might be gazing on her now: a prisoner watching her move between the bars of a cell's window; parted lovers gazing upon her at an agreed time, as though her light might heal their separation; some lone sailor, like Coleridge's Mariner, who 'yearneth towards the journeying Moon'.

The moon that I saw was waxing still, but almost at the full, and the sky in which she shone was almost cloudless, but she made me think of a passage that I half-remembered from Belloc's book *The Four Men*, about the time they see the moon together; although, as we discover, they are not four separate men at all, but four aspects of Belloc himself as he walks companionably with himself back into the Sussex of his childhood.

When I came back into the house, I looked up the passage: 'The sky was already of an apple green to the westward, and in the eastern blue there were stars. There also shone what had not yet appeared upon that windless day, a few small wintry clouds, neat and defined in heaven. Above them the moon, past her first quarter but not yet full, was no longer pale, but began to make a cold glory; and all that valley of Adur was a great and solemn sight to see as we went forward upon our adventure that led nowhere and away … All four of us together received the sacrament of that wide and silent beauty, and we ourselves went in silence to receive it.'

Rereading this passage on that moonlit night, I became aware that I owed Belloc an unacknowledged debt; for, earlier this year, working on my new Arthurian poems, in ballad form with 'skipping reels of rhyme', I was writing about the night vigil of Dindrane, the Grail Maiden who will eventually guide the knights on their quest. I realise now that my verse must have been informed unconsciously by some memory of Belloc's suggestive phrase 'the sacrament of that wide and silent beauty'; for this is what I wrote:

By night she kept pure vigil there
And morning came too soon
For she would see the stars wheel by
And hear their music from on high
And feel their influence and cry
In ecstasy, when she'd descry
A sphere of silver light draw nigh,
Then she would lift her eyes and spy
Above the valley's chalice high:
The wafer of the moon.

56

Seven Sunken Englands

Returning, after a long break, to work on my Arthurian ballads, I thought that I would read myself back into the form by revisiting G. K. Chesterton's great narrative poem about King Alfred, *The Ballad of the White Horse*. This time, I was especially struck by the dedicatory verses to his wife, Frances. In that dedication, he asks the obvious question: Why bother? Why should we try to retell these old stories, whether of legend or of history? Is it even possible, and, if it were, can it have anything to say to us now? As Chesterton puts it, rather more poetically:

> Why bend above a shapeless shroud
> Seeking in such archaic cloud
> Sight of strong lords and light?

He rephrases the question again in the next verse, but in such a way that the question begins to answer itself:

> Where seven sunken Englands
> Lie buried one by one,
> Why should one idle spade, I wonder,
> Shake up the dust of thanes like thunder
> To smoke and choke the sun?

That image of the 'seven sunken Englands' overlayed on top of one another is wonderfully suggestive. Indeed, rereading it suddenly called to mind a brilliant lecture I heard Rowan Williams give, years ago, to a gathering of the David Jones Society. Discussing the great Welsh poet's vision of the world and his poetic technique, Williams said that time, in Jones's writing, was not figured or experienced as an arrow flying past us, or a succession of streaming moments each carrying everything away irrevocably into the past. But, rather, Lord Williams suggested, time for Jones is like a series of layers richly accumulating over the same patch of ground, the same city or valley or hamlet. Like leaves accumulating on a forest floor, each successive year leaves a place more richly layered, more deeply patterned and textured. And all these layers of history and legend are still there, ready to be woken and evoked by the poet, ready to be made present again, and to give us a much fuller and more nuanced sense of who and where we are.

All that seemed implicit in Chesterton's phrase, as well as Jones's poetry, vastly different though the two poets are; for, where Jones gives us high-modernist prose-poetry, immensely learned in many languages, and bristling with footnotes, Chesterton offers a swinging, ringing, swashbuckling popular ballad, which helped many ordinary people to read and understand the times that lay ahead of them.

Although the poem was published in 1911, it accompanied and encouraged many soldiers in the First World War, and its phrases 'Naught for your comfort' and 'The High Tide and the Turn' were taken up in editorials in *The Times* during the Second World War.

Chesterton asks and answers one last vital question in his dedicatory poem:

But who shall look from Alfred's hood
Or breathe his breath alive?
His century like a small dark cloud
Drifts far …

Can we ever look out from the eyes of our ancestors and know the world as they knew it? Chesterton suggests that, for all the other changes and chances, if we share the same great creed as our forebears and see the world in the light of the cross and resurrection, then we can, indeed, see as they saw. Chesterton looks at the pendant cross that his wife is wearing and puts it like this:

> Lady, by one light only
> We look from Alfred's eyes,
> We know he saw athwart the wreck
> The sign that hangs about your neck,
> Where One more than Melchizedek
> Is dead and never dies.

57

Holding and Letting Go

It is only too true, as Socrates observed, that a poet is not necessarily the best judge of what is happening in their own poem, or what it is ultimately about. Poems are like children: you nurture and form them up to a certain point, and of course you have your own ideas about what they mean, and who they are.

But they are living, independent beings, and, like children growing up and leaving home, published poems go out and make their own way in the world. They make new friends and have conversations that their parents could never have imagined, and perhaps shouldn't overhear. But, sometimes, they come home with their new friends, and you have the pleasure of knowing that someone has seen something in your child, or in your poem, that you hadn't seen yourself, but you're very glad it's there.

I learned this most vividly when a poem, which I had thought was so personal that I might not publish it, went out anyway and found its own friends. It happened like this: I had intended to go with my father to the funeral of one of his old friends. My father was unwell, and we both had some sense of his mortality, too, of the precious time left to us.

At the last minute, I was called away to a pastoral crisis in my college, and couldn't go with him; but a friend of mine and his went with him instead. I glanced behind me as I set off for college, and saw that she had reached out to hold my father's hand as they walked to church. I was so grateful, and, later that day, I penned her a little poem. My wife asked if she could send the poem to a friend in Canada, who, in turn, unbeknown to me, shared it with a friend who worked in a hospice.

A week later, I got an email headed 'Your Hospice Poem'! I had no idea what this was about, but the email said: 'Thank you for the poem which so completely expresses our work and vision as a hospice, we would like to frame it on our wall and include it in our newsletter.' I was flummoxed. But it turned out to be the little poem that I had written for my friend and shown to Maggie.

When I reread the poem, I suddenly realised that they were right about it, and I was wrong. It really was their poem, a poem about something far more than I had in mind when I had inscribed it in a thank-you card for my friend. Here's how it went:

Holding and Letting Go

We have a call to live, and oh
A common call to die.
I watched you and my father go
To bid a friend goodbye.
I watched you hold my father's hand,
How could it not be so?
The gentleness of holding on
Helps in the letting go.

For when we feel our frailty
How can we not respond?
And reach to hold another's hand
And feel the common bond?
For then we touch the heights above
And every depth below,
We touch the very quick of love:
Holding and letting go.

58

A Coronation Psalm

I was away in America when I heard news of the Queen's death, and tears came to my eyes for the loss of someone whom I had never met, yet had been an unfailing presence, a reassurance and an example of servant leadership for the whole of my life.

I was relieved to know that I would be flying home that very evening, and that I would soon have my feet on the soil over which she was sovereign, and among the people she loved and served, who would know and share my grief.

And so I was at home to witness not only the mourning, and the many beautiful recollections and remembrances of her long and fruitful reign, but also His Majesty's moving address to the nation, the first singing of 'God Save the King', and the formal proclamation of our new sovereign.

Even as these great occasions of state are celebrated, the ordinary life of the Church and the nation goes on, but its very routines are sometimes lifted into a new light by this time of transition. So it was that, in my usual journey through the psalter, I came to Psalm 21, often referred to as a coronation psalm:

> The King shall rejoice in thy strength, O Lord: exceeding glad shall he be of thy salvation.
> Thou hast given him his heart's desire: and hast not denied him the request of his lips.
> For thou shalt prevent him with the blessings of goodness: and shalt set a crown of pure gold upon his head.

As I read it, I felt this psalm shimmering into new significance. Early Christians applied it to Christ 'the son of

David', and therefore the understanding of coronation itself deepened. Before he wears the golden crown prophesied in this psalm, Christ, the true Messiah, comes to suffer with his creation and to wear the crown of thorns, the *corona spinea*, as it was called in Latin. For the word *corona*, which we have learned to dread, is there in the word coronation, and is surely part of Christ's *corona spinea;* for he enters into our suffering that we might enter into his glory.

Turning back to my response to this psalm in *David's Crown*, I felt that this poem might serve as a prayer and blessing for these days between the grief of parting and the consolation of a new coronation:

Now may you find in Christ, riches *and* rest,
May you be blessed in him, and he in you
In Heaven, where to grant you your request

Is always blessing, for your heart is true:
True to yourself and true to Christ your king.
Breathe through this coronation psalm and view

The glory of his golden crown, then sing
The exaltation, goodness, life and power,
The blessing and salvation Christ will bring.

But first he wears a darker crown. The hour
Is coming and has come. Our Lord comes down
Into the heart of all our hurts to wear

The sharp *corona spinea*, crown
Of thorns, and to descend with us to death
Before he shares with us the golden crown.

59

At the Treacle Well

I have been walking with three friends on a riverside pilgrimage between Dorchester and Oxford. One of our pilgrim paths, from Oxford itself, took us across the lovely expanse of Port Meadow, out to Binsey – once an island, as its name suggests, with its ancient church dedicated to St Margaret of Antioch, but associated as much with another saint, who made the original dedication and built the church: St Frideswide, Oxford's patron saint. Our walk across the meadow and towards the Isis's lovely bank took us past the poplars and young beech trees that have, thankfully, been replanted to replace the ones whose loss Hopkins so memorably lamented:

> My aspens dear, whose airy cages quelled,
> Quelled or quenched in leaves the leaping sun,
> All felled, felled, are all felled …

But on our walk, we could still enjoy the way green trees

> … dandled a sandalled
> Shadow that swam or sank
> On meadow & river & wind-wandering weed-winding
>   bank.

Once we'd crossed the river, we came to a fingerpost with signs pointing in opposite directions, proclaiming their rhyming destinations: 'The Church' or 'The Perch'.

My fellow pilgrims and I had lunch in The Perch, and, suitably sustained and refreshed, returned to the sign and headed for the real object of our pilgrimage: the church and, more particularly, the holy well beside it, which goes by the happy name of 'The Treacle Well'.

This is indeed the famous Treacle Well from *Alice's Adventures in Wonderland*, where, according to the learned and somnolent Dormouse, three sisters lived entirely on treacle. But the real back story of the Treacle Well is even more wonderful.

The name derives from 'triacle', an Anglo-Saxon word for a healing balm or salve; and, the story goes, Frideswide, the Saxon princess who became the patron saint of Oxford, fled to the little isle of Binsey, on a boat rowed by angels, to escape the unwelcome advances of a Mercian king.

She hid in the woods there, and, as he attempted to pursue her further, he was struck blind for his sacrilege; for Frideswide was vowed to celibacy. But the Lord told her to touch the ground with her staff, and, where it touched, a miraculous spring flowed forth, and she had compassion on her oppressor, and, with the 'triacle' salve, she healed his blindness. She seems also to have healed his moral blindness; for she was able to return to Oxford and found a priory, but not before she had founded the church by the well and dedicated it in honour of St Margaret of Antioch, who had likewise fled an unwanted male pursuer.

It's an ancient tale, and yet it has, all too sadly, a modern ring to it. Perhaps Margaret and Frideswide – and, indeed, Etheldreda of Ely – might form an early sisterhood for the #MeToo movement; perhaps there was something in the Dormouse's assertion that the Treacle Well was a place where sisters dwelt together.

All these thoughts were revolving in my mind as I approached the well itself. I descended the steps and peered through a low arch to glimpse the water, deeper down in the well, and, when I saw it, I entirely understood Alice and the Dormouse; for, I must say, it did look exactly like treacle.

60

A Fish Out of Water?

The other week, I found myself in Nashville, in the magnificently named Gaylord Opryland Resort and Convention Centre. This was less like a hotel than like a hideously Disneyfied version of Coleridge's Xanadu in 'Kubla Khan'; for it did indeed seem that 'twice five miles of fertile ground, With walls and towers were girded round', and all that vast acreage was roofed over, although this was less a 'stately pleasure dome' and more a plastic one.

However far you walked, it was almost impossible to get outdoors: you would look down from a balcony or a high walkway and see the 'gardens bright with sinuous rills' and the 'sunny spots of greenery'; but then you would look up, and there was the ceiling with its glass panels, and all around was the whirr of the air-conditioning, the distant hum of hidden pumps and machinery.

Within this vast indoor space, there was even a river with cascades and waterfalls – a river so extensive that you could pay to have a boat tour on it. But it went only round in circles. It was scarcely 'Alph, the sacred river' from Coleridge's poem, that primal fount of poetic imagination welling eternally from the Eden within us. Rather, it was a sanitised replica that flowed between plastic banks and the faked paraphernalia of some idealised New Orleans. Even the tour boat, it turned out, didn't actually float, but ran on a little grooved track at the bottom of the 'river'. As far as the eye could see, everything (and perhaps everyone) was pretending to be something other than itself. No wonder I felt like a fish out of water.

I was just thinking this, standing on a little bridge over the water, when I noticed that there were real fish in the artificial river: huge catfish and outsized carp were swimming round and round the immense and inane circularity of that river. The Northern Irish artist Ross Wilson, who happened to be standing beside me, suddenly asked: 'Do you think those fish know this isn't real?' It was a great question, just the kind that artists are apt to ask. For a second, I imagined archangels, supercelestial intelligences, leaning over the edge of heaven and gazing down on the two of us, lost in these shadowlands, and asking: 'Do you think they know it's not real?'

And yet, for all the tackiness of our surroundings, we were also immersed in something real and very revitalising: a celebration of church music, hymnody and song, and, by extension, of the interplay between theology and the imaginative arts. Not all the music was to my taste, but it was all excellently done, with heart and soul, as well as skill. When several thousand people all began to sing harmonies, it was abundantly beautiful: a touch of the 'symphony and song' in Coleridge's poem.

I was there as poet-in-residence, and, that evening, I had the joy of standing on the stage of the 'Grand Ole Opry', among musicians I deeply admired, and reciting my own encomium on music, in some lines from my 'Ode to St Cecilia':

Cecilia, give way to grace again,
Transmute it into music for us all:
Music to stir and call the sleeping soul,
And set a counterpoint to all our pain,
To bless our senses in their very essence
And undergird our sorrow in good ground.
Music to summon undeserved abundance,
Unlooked-for over-brimming, rich and strong;
The unexpected plenitude of sound
Becoming song.

125

61

On Lindisfarne

I have been briefly back to beloved Northumbria, and, in particular, back on to the Holy Island of Lindisfarne. Like Iona, whence Aidan came to found the monastery on Lindisfarne, the island is one of 'the thin places', as they have been called: places where the veil between heaven and earth is thinner, where the light of the eternal shimmers through the veil of time and place.

In some ways, it's a helpful phrase, but it's also misleading. It might seem to suggest that the outer and earthly is dismissed, or becomes more vague and less substantial because it is in some sense displaced by the glimmers of heaven, the 'intimations of immortality' which shine through it.

But this is not my experience. On the contrary, there seems something in the very quality of the light up there, as it diffuses from clouds and lifts from the sea, which gives wonderful focus, almost a hyper-reality, to everything that I see: the shining pebbles on the shore, the individual grains of sand, all the singular-shaped stones in the ruined priory.

I become intensely aware of 'the minute particulars', as Blake called them in his visionary poem *Jerusalem*: 'He who wishes to see a Vision; a perfect Whole, Must see it in its Minute Particulars.'

And, again, where Los, the figure of the Artist in that poem says: 'Labour well the Minute Particulars, attend to the Little-ones.'

We don't glimpse heaven in a thin place because the earth is dim, but precisely because all the earthly things, in their minute particulars, shine with heaven's light.

It is this loving attention to the tiny detail in light of the cosmic whole which is at the heart of the art of the Lindisfarne Gospels; and I was on the island as part of a celebration of the return of that precious book to the north. There has been, in these past two weeks, a pilgrimage in St Cuthbert's footsteps and in the footsteps of Cuthbert's people, who carried the holy body from the depredations of the Viking raids, till eventually it was brought to rest in Durham.

But this pilgrimage reversed the journey and brought a replica of his coffin, of the Lindisfarne Gospels and of the Cuthbert Gospel, the beautiful little Gospel of John that was found on Cuthbert's breast when the coffin was opened – brought all these treasures back to the island that first gave birth to and nurtured them. I was there to read poems both about Cuthbert and about his Gospel to the pilgrims as they gathered in the ancient church of St Mary.

I was there only for an evening, as the tide allowed, but I have stayed on the island when it is truly an island, when the returning waters have covered the causeway and set us free from the rush of things and all the land's long cares. Indeed, there is something apt and fruitful about the island's rhythm and interplay between being a true island and being once more 'a part of the main'.

John Donne was right to say that 'No man is an island, entire of itself; every man is a piece of the continent, a part of the main'; but it is also true that we sometimes need a little isolation on some inner *insula sacra*, a place of solitude, to renew those springs that will later flow back into the world; that we need, in Merton's phrase, 'contemplation in a world of action'.

The beautiful rhythm of the alternating tides around Lindisfarne, daily withdrawing and reconnecting, is a perfect emblem of that pattern in spiritual life; and, that evening, I was more than glad of my island moment.

62

The Fascination with What's Difficult

Someone asked me the other day why it is that, in an age of 'free verse', I submit, *contra mundum*, to the constraints of form; why I impose on myself the task of weighing words, ordering stress and accent into metrical pattern, finding rhyme.

There are many answers to that question. One is quite simply that form is beautiful in itself, that the patterning of language into sonnet and sestina summons the music of language itself, and that I am seeking to recover the lost music of English poetry, the music that sounded so richly and harmoniously in the poetry of Keats and Tennyson. I want to sound that music again, but with a contemporary voice.

But there is more to it than that. The Elizabethan poet Samuel Daniel, who influenced Shakespeare and many later poets, wrote the fine *Defense of Rhyme*, in which he speaks of the musicality of language itself: 'Every language hath her proper number or measure fitted to use and delight, which, Custom entertaining by the allowance of the Ear, doth indenize, and make natural. All verse is but a frame of words confined within certain measure; differing from the ordinary speech, and introduced, the better to express men's conceits, both for delight and memory.'

But he goes on to say something even more significant about the poet's actual experience of composing verse in this way – about the central paradox that these self-imposed restraints in fact introduce new freedoms and new possibilities: 'Rhyme is no impediment to his [the Poet's] conceit, but rather gives him wings to mount, and carries him, not out of his course, but as it were beyond his power to a far happier flight. All excellences being sold us at the hard price of labour, it follows, where we bestow most thereof, we buy the best success: and Rhyme, being far more laborious than loose measures (whatsoever is objected) must needs, meeting with wit and industry, breed greater and worthier effects in our language.'

I could not agree more, and I love the implicit metaphor, in the phrase 'give him wings to mount', of the muse as Pegasus, the winged steed, whose footprint on Mount Parnassus loosed the stream of Helicon, the archetypal fount of inspiration.

There is something of the same allusion in Yeats's fascinating and difficult poem 'The Fascination of What's Difficult'. In that poem, as he wrestles with the sheer drudgery and difficulty of writing his plays for the Abbey Theatre, he realises that, although Pegasus is Olympian, sky-born and magical, there are times when riding him is also a matter of drudgery and management:

> There's something ails our colt
> That must, as if it had not holy blood
> Nor on Olympus leaped from cloud to cloud,
> Shiver under the lash, strain, sweat and jolt
> As though it dragged road metal.

If poets who have chosen the constraint and form, ultimately finding that such service is also perfect freedom, have sometimes still to 'strain, sweat and jolt', then such experience may also be true of those other vocations that cannot simply indulge in self-expression, but must submit to a discipline, follow a form, and serve an art or a community that is more than themselves.

The priest who serves the liturgy, the pastor serving their flock, the teacher working within the constraints of classroom and curriculum – all of them submit to constraints that sometimes seem impossible and yet, 'meeting with wit and industry', produce something 'greater and worthier' than unconstrained and possibly self-indulgent self-expression could ever do.

63

A Few Gleanings

They've harvested the field of wheat alongside which I walk every day, for my path lies between the long field and the river, and just as Tennyson observed in *The Lady of Shallot*:

On either side the river lie.
Long fields of barley and of rye

Or, in this case, fields of wheat. I've watched it through all its changes, from the sown seed in the dark bare earth (some of it fallen on the pathway and snatched by the birds), through to the first tender shoots of green, then the rich green carpet, at first like grass, but soon growing steady and sturdy, and then, most beautiful of all, the gradual change in this last month, from green to gold, that rich gold, brighter under dark skies, of the field ready for harvest, the kind of glowing, numinous gold that Samuel Palmer, and latterly Roger Wagner have so excelled in painting. And now, as I walk alongside the field all that golden grain is harvested. Yet the harvester did not take everything, for all along the field side path are many heads of grain still on their stalks, good gleaning for anyone who needs them. I pick up a golden stalk and rub it in my hands, the chaff falling easily from the grain and blowing away, and I feel as though I had the whole gospel, with all its long reach back into earlier scripture, lying open in the palm of my hand.

Here are just such field-edge gleanings as Boaz left for Ruth, that she might, in Heaney's phrase, 'glean the unsaid off the palpable' and understand her welcome, and that together they might begin that line of descent that led down to David and beyond. And so they first made sacred the little town of Bethlehem, so that in Bethlehem, 'the house of bread', the Bread of Life might be born. And here in my hand were just such 'heads of grain' as Jesus and his disciples once plucked on a sabbath to stave off hunger, citing David as their precedent, and such a grain of wheat as Jesus, looking at his disciples, might have let fall to the ground through his fingers when he spoke of his coming passion and said to them, 'Very truly, I tell you, unless a grain of wheat falls into the earth and dies, it remains just a single grain; but if it dies, it bears much fruit.'

And here, as I let the grains fall through my fingers back to the good earth, was the golden field all harvested, already gathered into barns, a sign of that final fruition, that harvest-home at the end of time which will begin our true life and such rejoicing as every harvest feast faintly anticipates.

I'm glad of these continuities in seed-time and harvest, glad to see the bread of life golden in the field before its wrapped in plastic in the shops, and glad to live in a place where my daily walks can give me little insights, small gleanings perhaps, of all the richer meanings embedded in the language of scripture when it is also the language of nature.

64

A Door In and Out

'A book is a door in, and therefore a door out!' So says the Raven in *Lilith*, George MacDonald's remarkable fantasy, first published in 1895, and published again this year in a new edition of his collected works. This book, together with his earlier novel *Phantastes*, certainly proved to be a door into the world of luminous symbolic fantasy writing for authors such as C. S. Lewis and J. R. R. Tolkien, and, more recently, for Ursula Le Guin, Susanna Clarke and many others.

MacDonald showed that, once we willingly suspended our disbelief and entered into an author's magical realm – a secondary world, a 'sub-creation', as Tolkien called it – then we could be taken out of ourselves, out of our contemporary routines and assumptions, and immersed in an imaginary world through whose atmosphere, images and stories we are given an entirely new perspective. And, more crucially, he showed that we would take the door out from that imaginary world back into our own, strengthened, encouraged and given new wisdom and insight.

Lilith itself is a fantasy that takes us out of our own world into another, and yet every detail of that other multidimensional world is, as MacDonald calls it, a 'live thought': every image is an emblem that speaks of more than itself, one that becomes an image with which and through which we can think.

Lilith is a strange and fantastical book. A librarian whom we meet at the beginning of the novel turns out to be a raven in the otherworld, but also, when we press deeper, he is Adam, and we will also meet Eve, and Lilith herself, a figure in Mesopotamian and Judaic mythology who is supposed to have been Adam's first wife. In MacDonald's era, she was the subject of both a poem and a painting by D. G. Rossetti, and, in MacDonald's fantasy, she represents our fear of death – indeed, our fear of every little death, every form of letting go.

MacDonald's Lilith is the one who most deeply resists, and yet finally learns to accept, the primal pattern of death and resurrection; for even the darkest images in this strange novel, like the worms that wisdom's raven beak draws out from the soil of our subconscious, are flung up into the light and grow wings. From the great archetypes of Adam, Eve and Lilith to the resonant and suggestive landscapes, the dry water courses beneath which, nevertheless, the water of life still flows; from the simple cottages where bread and wine are a transformative sacrament to the decaying palaces where every luxury is an empty corruption; from the live forest where the trees themselves and the birds of the air are living thoughts and prayers to the desolate and cruel city awaiting its transformation, every image in this book has a power of suggestion, of incipient symbol, which will challenge and deepen the reader's self-understanding.

Not that any of these images are, in any sense, frigid allegory; on the contrary, this is, as Lewis affirmed, mythopoeic writing of the highest order. MacDonald is not squeezing pre-digested thoughts into some symbolic code, but, rather, letting the symbols themselves – the story itself – do their own work on us and in us, constantly suggesting and generating new insights.

The new edition of *Lilith* has illustrations by Gabrielle Ragusi, the contemporary Italian illustrator of fantasy and science fiction, which could help to bring this seminal and generative novel to a whole new generation. Who knows what future Lewis or Tolkien might first have their imagination aroused and then baptised here?

65

An Unveiling

I am just back from the unveiling of a beautiful new statue of Samuel Taylor Coleridge, in his home town of Ottery St Mary. It was a glorious occasion, timed for the 250th anniversary of his birth, and the event drew admirers of the poet and his work from all over England and beyond, and also saw the gathering of many of his direct descendants and members of the wider Coleridge family.

I was especially moved by the fact that the statue depicts the young Coleridge in the prime of his life, as an ardent visionary, and already a profound philosopher, not indoors in his study, but out fell-walking, balanced on a rocky outcrop, notebook in hand gazing upward and outward. He looks just as he must have when he climbed Scafell Pike and made those thrilling notebook entries which also sealed his claim to be the first English mountaineer. It's a beautiful work of art, and, surprisingly, the first full-size statue of the poet.

I spoke to the sculptor, Nicholas Dimbleby, and it was clear that he had entered into the full Coleridgean spirit in making the piece. For this is no static monument, with its two feet resting equally on some solid and imperturbable plinth, but a figure in motion, ascending, balancing weight on an upper foot as the lower lifts to continue the movement upwards.

Achieving such a sense of movement was a huge technical challenge, the sculptor told me, and the great piece of boulder from which the poet leans forward is as much a part of the sculpture as the bronze figure itself.

The other remarkable thing is the location of the statue: just outside the church, still within its grounds, still on consecrated soil. This not only reflects the poet's early links with the church where his father was vicar: the churchyard, where the statue now stands, was the scene of the poet's first reveries on nature and of his ardent daydreaming. It also speaks of the way that the mature Coleridge returned to the roots of his Christian faith, and rediscovered the deepest truths of the gospel made fresh and compelling in the light of his distinct theology of the Imagination, as a necessary complement to the work of Reason.

As he said in the conclusion to his *Biographia Literaria*: 'Christianity, as taught in the Liturgy and Homilies of our Church, though not discoverable by human Reason, is yet in accordance with it; that link follows link by necessary consequence; that Religion passes out of the ken of Reason only where the eye of Reason has reached its own Horizon; and that Faith is then but its continuation ...'

It has sometimes been remarked that Coleridge's theology, his imaginative and symbolic reading of scripture, was too far in advance of the Church of his day to be fully appreciated. That may be so, but, as eco-poet and prophet, and as a theologian who calls and recalls us to wonder and to the depths of symbol, he has become, with every passing generation, a more prophetic, and indeed a more contemporary voice.

When we turned from the unveiling, and went back into the church, we heard a sermon from one of the successors of Coleridge's father, the present Team Rector, the Revd Lydia Cook. She drew so succinctly and comprehensively on Coleridge's best theology, and applied it so well to our time, that I had real hope that the Church of England is at last catching up with one of its greatest luminaries.

66

With Alfred at Wantage

I have been staying this week in Wantage, as a guest of the Community of St Mary the Virgin, where I am leading a retreat. It is a beautiful and restful place, nestled into the Vale of the White Horse. Although this was my first visit, the community of Sisters here had already done me a great deal of good; for the first time I saw that the letters 'C.S.M.V.' were on the cover of a beautiful lucid translation of St Athanasius's little book on the incarnation, which was translated by 'A Religious of C.S.M.V.'

That 'religious' was none other than Sister Penelope, a great scholar and translator of both Greek and Latin texts, including a lovely version of St Bernard on the Song of Songs. She was a remarkable woman, and corresponded and exchanged manuscripts with both C. S. Lewis and Thomas Merton.

That little book on the incarnation was one of the important stepping-stones for me on my journey back to a full Christian faith, as was the brilliant introduction to it by Lewis. Indeed, Lewis became a great friend of Sister Penelope, and they had a long correspondence. He dedicated *Perelandra*, obliquely, to the Community, with the inscription 'To Some Ladies at Wantage'. As he noted wryly to Sister Penelope in a letter, that dedication somehow came out, in a Portuguese translation, as 'To some wanton ladies'!

I was leading a retreat on the Psalms, but, on Wednesday, they invited me to celebrate communion, and it happened to be the day set aside to remember and celebrate King Alfred, 'a local saint', as they informed me with some pride. That afternoon, I wandered into Wantage itself, and there, in the little Market Square, I saw the fine statue of Alfred the

Great, its white stone almost glowing in the autumn sunshine. Stepping a little closer, I read the inscription on the base of the statue:

Alfred Found Learning Dead
And He Restored It.
Education Neglected
And He Revived It.
The Laws Powerless
And He Gave Them Force.
The Church Debased
And He Raised It.
The Land Ravaged By A Fearful enemy
From Which He Delivered It.

Even as we lurched, yet again, between governments, between prime ministers, between all the specious promises and vague clichés of our present political discourse, I couldn't help giving a wistful sigh as I read that inscription; for so much in our realm at present is neglected, so many are powerless, so much is debased or debilitated by the recent ravages of both plague and war, as it was when Alfred began his programme of reform and renewal.

If a new administration, whether before or after a General Election, could propose and achieve even half of what the great Wessex king did, we would have every reason to be thankful.

I was glad that, at the morning eucharist, the Sisters had invoked Alfred's aid and intercession for the nation. We're going to need it.

67

Steeped in Ireland

I have been spending a day or two amid the beauties of Northern Ireland, along the Antrim coast, with its Giant's Causeway and tantalising glimpses of Scotland across the water, and also, a little inland, in Coleraine, on the banks of the beautiful river Bann, where I was speaking at a C. S. Lewis conference put on by the University of Ulster.

It was a fitting place to celebrate and explore Lewis's works; for he was, and often affirmed himself to be, an Irishman, and, within that broader identity, more specifically, an Ulsterman.

Of course, when Lewis was born in Belfast in 1898, and, indeed, for the first 23 years of his life, Ireland was still united. When, as a teenager, he wrote enthusiastically to his Belfast friend Arthur Greeves about having discovered the poetry of Yeats, he said: 'Here is a poet who really loves *our* mythology.'

But, even after partition, Lewis still referred to himself simply as 'Irish'. When he was recording the talks that became *The Four Loves* for an American audience, one of the producers queried his breathing and intonation. Lewis replied: 'I'm Irish, not English. Did you ever know an Irishman who did not puff and blow?'

More seriously, and with more particular nuance, he once disagreed with an Oxford student's praise of Cromwell, because he shared the collective folk memory of the massacre Cromwell perpetrated at Drogheda, saying: 'You see, I'm an Irishman. Yes, Northern Irish, but that makes it worse; the offenders you can't forgive are the ones on your own side.'

The conference in Coleraine was very much alive to the nuances and particularities of Lewis's Irish identity – not just politically (Lewis was a 'Home Ruler' and quarrelled with his father, who was a Unionist), but also, and perhaps more importantly for Lewis, the influence of those mutually enfolded miracles of language and landscape.

Lewis loved the Irish landscape, particularly the beauties of Donegal (for which he invented the special word 'Donegality'), but also the Carlingford Mountains in County Louth, especially where those mountains overlooked Carlingford Loch, a landscape that, Lewis once said, 'most resembled Narnia'. Indeed, his hand-drawn map of Narnia, made to guide his illustrator Pauline Baynes, resembles quite closely the county and coastline of Louth, with Cair Paravel sited where Louth has its twelfth-century King John's Castle, a place where the first drafts of Magna Carta were begun.

There were linguistic experts at the conference, delighting us with some of the felicities of 'Ulster Scots' as a dialect, and also, a wonderful surprise, we heard a reading from *The Lion, the Witch and the Wardrobe*, as it has been translated into Irish, and not just generic Irish, but its specifically Ulster variants. The reader of that translation told us that the common term for a large wardrobe in those parts, in both languages, was a linen press; indeed, if you were to retranslate that book back out of Ulster Irish into English, its title would read *The Lion, the Witch and the Linen Press*.

The day after the conference, I made my own pilgrimage to another special site – for me, at least: the magnificent Bushmills Distillery. On the tour, they explained how the distinct and subtle flavours of the whiskey were acquired over many years, from the particular woods of the barrels that they matured in. I, for one, will now feel more able to savour the distinctive flavours of the Irish landscape and language in which Lewis was steeped for so many years.

68

The Wind in the Trees

I have been out and enjoying our windy autumn weather. I always feel a surge of excitement when a big gust comes, and I exalt in the 'wild west wind, the breath of autumn's being', as Shelley called it in his exhilarating Ode. It's especially thrilling when one approaches woodland in a big wind, and so it was for me, pushing my way through the gusts as I climbed Rivey Hill and approached the ancient woodland that clothes its summit. The closer I got, the louder came the roar of the wind in the trees. It's an extraordinary sound: if you close your eyes it might be the roar and pounding of waves in a storm and you have the momentarily dislocating eeriness of the sound of the sea above you! I didn't go into the woods themselves, as I could imagine not only 'the dead leaves driven like ghosts from an enchanter fleeing / yellow and black and pale and hectic red' but also, in this wind, great branches flying and falling, and perhaps even one or two of the trees coming down, so I skirted the top of the wood and simply savoured the sound. As I walked I found it was not only Shelley's Ode, but something far older, that came to my mind: the rhythmic cadences of Coverdale's version of Psalm 29 from the BCP: 'The voice of the Lord breaketh the cedar-trees: yea, the Lord breaketh the cedars of Libanus. He maketh them also to skip like a calf: Libanus also, and Sirion, like a young unicorn.'

Earlier on this year it gave me great pleasure to make my own poetic response to that psalm in *David's Crown*, the psalm-poems I have been writing, and I realised that the poetic form of *Terza Rima*, which I had chosen for that sequence, was in fact the same form that Shelley had used in the *Ode to the West Wind*. In my poem though, I wanted more than the great voice of the wind in the trees, the rivers in full spate and the thunder. I also wanted the voice of conscience; and more than that, the voice of compassion that seems to speak from the very wounds of Christ. The poem came out like this:

XXIX *Afferte Domino*

Call us, O Christ, and open up the gate.
Call us to worship with your mighty voice:
The voice that sings through rivers in full spate,

The voice in which the forests all rejoice,
The voice that rolls through thunderclouds, and calls
The deep seas and steep waves, the quiet voice

That stirs our sleeping conscience and recalls
Us to the love we had abandoned, leads
Us through the parting mists of doubt, or falls

Upon us like a revelation, pleads
With us upon the poor's behalf, blazes
In glory from each burning bush, and bleeds

Out from compassion's wounds, raises
Our spirits till we dance for joy
And gives us too, a voice to sing his praises.

69

Rereading 'Eden Rock'

I have been dipping again into the collected poems of Charles Causley, the Poet Laureate we never had, both for sheer pleasure and also because Causley was a modern master of the ballad form – reinventing, reinvigorating it, and putting it to good contemporary use. I am using the ballad form myself for my Arthurian poems, and I hoped to sit at the feet of a master and learn.

But, aside from the ballads I was revisiting, I found again his almost perfect poem, 'Eden Rock', written when he was in his seventies. It went through me with all its clarity, its shy slant rhymes, and the sudden joyful shock of its ending, as though I were reading it for the first time. It is marvellous how a poem can be so specific and detailed, and yet so capable, as all poetry should be, of gesturing beyond itself. It starts, familiarly, disarmingly enough:

> They are waiting for me somewhere beyond Eden Rock:
> My father, twenty-five, in the same suit
> Of Genuine Irish Tweed, his terrier Jack
> Still two years old and trembling at his feet.
>
> My mother, twenty-three, in a sprigged dress
> Drawn at the waist, ribbon in her straw hat,
> Has spread the stiff white cloth over the grass.
> Her hair, the colour of wheat, takes on the light.

You see the images so clearly that you hardly notice the deft music of the poem working on you in its hidden way: the way 'dress' is picked up and half echoed by 'grass' and 'hat' by light, the 'nearly but not quite' of the half rhymes taking on the suggestive otherness of the phrase 'somewhere beyond' in the opening line.

The poem goes on to describe his two parents setting out a picnic for three, his mother pouring tea out of a Thermos into the three 'tin cups painted blue'. And then she 'shades her eyes and looks my way, Over the drifted stream.' And it dawns on the reader that this is more than memory. And then comes that final verse with its last line set apart, floating beyond the rest of the stanza:

> They beckon to me from the other bank.
> I hear them call, 'See where the stream-path is!
> Crossing is not as hard as you might think.'

I had not thought that it would be like this.

Suddenly, you find yourself rereading the whole poem in a new light. Andrew Motion once said that if he could write a line as perfect as the one which closes this poem, he would go to his grave a happy man.

I called Causley 'the Poet Laureate we never had' because he was, in fact, considered for the post in the year that Ted Hughes became Laureate, and Hughes himself said later: 'Before I was made Poet Laureate, I was asked to name my choice of the best poet for the job. Without hesitation, I named Charles Causley.' Hughes went on to say: 'I was pleased to hear that in an unpublished letter, Philip Larkin thought the same and chose him too.'

I am sure that Causley has his laurel leaves now, on the other side of that stream.

70

In the Woods

Most mornings, I walk into the woods, and, in a clearing in their midst, I pause to contemplate, or smoke a pipe, or both. Brief gleams of fugitive November sunlight occasionally break through the clouds and light the lichen-covered boles of the trees, adding a gleam of gold to their rich deep green; and, sometimes, a pool of light briefly blesses the red and gold carpet of birch leaves, and they shimmer like spilled treasure. I try to hold the moment, to absorb something of the stillness of the trees that stand around me, to enter into what Wendell Berry, in one of his 'Sabbath Poems', calls their 'standing Sabbath':

> Another Sunday morning comes
> And I resume the standing Sabbath
> Of the woods, where the finest blooms
> Of time return ...

But, even as I savour the moment, it slips away. I know I shouldn't follow it, but should remain, if I can, in 'the now'. In one of the *Screwtape Letters*, C. S. Lewis writes about the way we live in time, and are tempted out of the only reality, which is the present moment, tempted to dwell in nostalgia for the past or fear for the future; but, as Lewis says, 'The past is frozen and no longer flows, but the present is all lit up with golden rays, the present is the point at which time touches eternity.'

I wonder whether he was thinking of Boethius (one of his favourite authors), who speaks of eternity not as an endless iteration of minutes, but as a *nunc stans*, an eternal now. That, I sense, is part of what Wendell Berry meant by that memorable phrase 'the *standing* Sabbath of the woods'. He plays, of course, on the fact that the trees themselves stand to their sabbath, but also, perhaps, on the idea that their sabbath, unlike ours, 'stands' and does not retreat, but remains, as they stand giving God glory, and he, in his eternal Sabbath, contemplates them, and proclaims that they and his whole creation are good.

But for us, alas, the moment 'in and out of time', as Eliot called it, comes and goes, and we are left with 'the waste sad time, stretching before and after'.

When, in my sequence *David's Crown*, I came to write my response to Psalm 137, the great lament of exile, I didn't know till I began to which sense of exile I would respond; but it turned out to be the exile from eternity, which is part of our experience of time, for we live *super flumina*, and 'time, like an ever-rolling stream, bears all its sons away':

CXXXVII *Super flumina*

That we might find in Christ complete assurance
We still recall these stories of the past,
For in them is the pattern and persistence

Of our long exile from the things that last.
For we live *super flumina*: time flows
Away from us, and all we prize is lost

The moment we attain it, like the rose
That shows eternity yet fades and falls.
So all our songs and music still disclose

The tragedy of time. The voice that calls
Us from eternity must always make
An elegy. We beat against time's walls,

For this is Babylon. Our captors take
The best in us the moment it is born.
But Babylon will fall! We will awake!

71

A Debt to David Scott

Like many, I mourn the passing of David Scott, but I am immensely thankful that his memory and his poetry still abide. I owe him a personal as well as a literary debt. I met him during my troubled teenage years, when he became the only chaplain at Haberdashers' to take an interest in and care for the small group of boys cooped up in the great day school's neglected boarding house.

At the time, I was fiercely atheist, and took the opportunity of my encounters with him to try and trounce his faith. I had become obsessed with Samuel Beckett, and I remember reciting bits of Beckett at him, as though the mere existence of *Waiting for Godot* was sufficient to finish Christianity for ever.

His response was both unexpected and disarming. 'Ah, Malcolm,' he said. 'I'm so glad you've discovered Beckett, that Desert Father of the High Modernists.' Of course, I didn't know what a Desert Father was, and had to ask. He put the right books in my hands, and it was a strangely moving experience to read their lives and sayings, as though these ragged figures shared a stage with Estragon and Vladimir.

I came back for more, and David and I became good friends. We stayed in touch after I left school, and he showed me what I most wanted to know: that Christianity was a living faith, and that poetry and priesthood were real vocations. He showed me how one might live both within the poetic tradition and within the two great poems of liturgy and scripture; and yet still be open to all the nuances and complexities, the doubts and perturbations of contemporary life.

We also shared, it turned out, a deep and formative interest, amounting to veneration, in Lancelot Andrewes, and he gave me the beautiful translations he made of Andrewes's private prayers, which were renewed in David's deft re-imagining, as contemporary poems.

Now I open again the pages of the worn copy of *Playing for England*, which he inscribed for me so many years ago; and poem after poem speaks to me in his gentle searching voice. As I vest for a service, his little poem about the surplice comes back to me. I hear him say:

> For me it is my only finery, by law
> decent and comely; a vestry friend
> put on often in dread; given away
> to old deft fingers to mend.

And, on funeral days, I remember his glimpse of the surplice

> chucked on the back seat of the car
> with the purple stole and the shopping.

In some ways, his poetry has been like that for me: both a beautiful, time-honoured clothing, and also a companion in the midst of the everyday. What he says of the surplice in the last lines of that poem also stands for and summons the two traditions, spiritual and poetic, that his life and poetry have helped me to inhabit:

> We have put these garments on for centuries.
> They persist. We wither and crease inside them.

72

A Winter's Ale

November sees the nights get darker, but not just the nights, for me it is the ales that darken too. It's too early yet for the first proper Winter Ale Festivals, but not too early to seek out the 'Winter Warmers' that breweries start selling at this time of year, when Hopback's *Summer Lightening* gives way to ales with names like *Rudyard Ruby*, *Colton Coffee Stout*, *Funnel Blower* and *Deer Stalker*.

These should be enjoyed at leisure in front of a good log fire in a stone-flagged, dark-raftered inn, after a brisk winter walk with a few close friends who have tall stories to tell. But even if one is confined to quarters by Covid or other unforeseen vicissitudes, a good dark ale opened at home and slowly savoured can soothe the day and enliven the evening. Many of these dark ales are much stronger, some of them almost barley wines, and they ask to be savoured slowly. They are conducive to quiet reflection, warm reminiscence, and something of that *Otium Sacrum*, the holy leisure, which the old monasteries were founded to preserve.

So I was especially pleased when a friend gave me a bottle of *Tint Meadow*, an English Trappist ale, to take home and try. I had enjoyed various Belgian Trappist beers but didn't know there was an English one, and this was all the better, as Mount Saint Bernard, where it is brewed, is a place I have visited and whose life of prayer and wonderfully rich and quiet atmosphere I greatly admire.

I left it on a kitchen shelf for a while to settle and when the right time came took it out and poured it gently, for these ales are all 'live' and ferment a second time in the bottle itself and one must dispense them carefully so as not to cloud the ale with the leavings of the yeast.

It was superb: rich, dark, full of flavour, and so strong that I was content with the slow savouring of the one bottle all evening. It was only in the midst of that savouring that I actually read the rubric on the bottle about how it should be stored and served. In my experience these instructions are all the same – store in a cool dark place and pour gently – but the monks of Mount Saint Bernard had added something to that mantra: 'Store in a cool, dark, *quiet* place!' *Quiet!* I thought that was just wonderful – even the beer, like the monks who brew it, must enter into the Great Silence! I thought of my own visit to Mount Saint Bernard, of how restorative it had been for me to drink the silence in, and now, in another sense, I could drink it in again. I also felt a little twinge of guilt that I hadn't read the label earlier. Alas, our kitchen shelf is not always a quiet place, and I hoped my ale had not been too disturbed by George's insistent barking at feeding time, by the clatter and the chatter of our own meal preparations, or by *The Archers* when it was Maggie's turn to wash up, and Van Morrison, or the Grateful Dead when it was mine.

But savouring the last dark drop, I felt the monks' good brew had survived the ordeal. I did resolve, however, to get in a few more bottles to store in a greater silence and try again. Just by way of experiment!

73

A Scion of the Sheltering Tree

There's an old wooden umbrella stand by our front door
with a fine selection of walking sticks and staves that Maggie
and I have acquired over the years, each associated with the
place we acquired it and further garnished and enriched
with memories of all the walks, long and short, on which
that particular stick has assisted and accompanied us. There
are a couple of taller sticks from Northumberland, their horn
handles curved over like shepherd's crooks, one of which is
carved beautifully into the head of a bird, bending down to
preen its own neck. There are shorter, stouter, more work-a-
day sticks, each springing down from fine round firm balls
of wood, polished now like conkers or the smooth round
bowls of one of my brier pipes, but once the densely knotted
boles of wood from which the sticks originally sprung and
grew. I selected one such yesterday, a fine old cherry stick,
worn by the years, to accompany me as a familiar friend,
up over the brow of Rivey Hill and into the woods, taking
it back as it were to its source, back to see its living cousins,
still rooted in the earth and growing.

Pausing in the woods, and leaning on my stick, I found
myself remembering Leigh Hunt's wonderful, quirky encomium of sticks, in one of his finest familiar essays from
The Indicator: A Miscellany for the Fields and the Fireside.
His description of his own cherry stick might well be a
description of mine:

> We protest against this injustice done to sticks, those use-
> ful and once flourishing sons of a good old stock. Take,
> for instance, a common cherry stick, which is one of the
> favourite sort. In the first place, it is a very pleasant sub-

stance to look at, the grain running round it in glossy and shadowy rings. Then it is of primaeval antiquity, handed down from scion to scion through the most flourishing of genealogical trees.

I love the way he gives his stick a lineage, going back not just to the tree from which it sprang but deep into the long history of sticks and stick carrying.

As I wandered on through the woods, employing my stick every so often to clear the nettles in front of my path or assist me up and down the steep banks and over the little rivulets that run through that wood, I reflected on another lineage, another tradition, another kind of genealogical tree, and that is the tradition of the English Familiar Essay itself. It has its roots in the first translations of the essays of Montaigne, that personal, friendly, unbuttoned and familiar fireside tone which was then taken up in *The Spectator* by Steele and Addison, refined and polished by Johnson in *The Rambler* and then given fresh life and vigour, and occasionally a little passionate swagger by the great generation of the romantic essayists: Hazlitt, Lamb, De Quincy, and Leigh Hunt himself. It was Lamb who said that friendship is a sheltering tree, and a sense of personal friendship with the author is what characterises the familiar essay. Perhaps each individual essay is like a companionable walking stick plucked from the great sheltering tree of the tradition. For the tradition is still alive and growing. It developed on from those romantics and flourished in the hands of Chesterton and Belloc, of Orwell and so many others. Even this little column, in its own small way, is a slender scion of that mighty, sheltering tree.

74

Rereading Keats

I have been rereading the odes of Keats, or perhaps I should say 're-chanting them'. I know them by heart anyway, though I love to see them on the page, especially in a finely printed book, and even as I read them I can't help chanting them out, for part of their power is in the very way they sound, delicious and mellifluous, to be tasted on the palate like the claret Keats loved. Indeed re-chanting them really means re-enchanting them, and then, with the spell of these poems, re-enchanting the world around us. The world is always somehow richer and more vivid when you're reading Keats, and not only while you're reading, but for a long while afterwards. You never really know how tender is the night until you read the *Ode to a Nightingale* and wander out afterwards and see for yourself 'the queen moon on her throne, clustered around by all her starry fays'. But the ode that has particularly entranced, or re-entranced, me recently is the *Ode on Melancholy*, and once more I find that the Covid lockdown brings an old poem into new focus. Perhaps there's always some undertow of melancholy in all of us, but we feel it all the more in the midst of this world-sorrow. The question is what to do with it? How to manage it? And here Keats comes to our aid, for his advice is neither to over-indulge nor to ignore it, but to bring it to beauty. So he begins his Ode with the memorable warning:

> No, no, go not to Lethe, neither twist
>   Wolf's-bane, tight-rooted, for its poisonous wine;
> You must not let the dark things become:
> A partner in your sorrow's mysteries;
>   For shade to shade will come too drowsily,
>   And drown the wakeful anguish of the soul.

His advice instead, 'when the melancholy fit shall fall', is this:

> Then glut thy sorrow on a morning rose,
>   Or on the rainbow of the salt sand-wave,
>   Or on the wealth of globed peonies …

And he is right. Many people have found on their solitary walks that it is the rich beauty of the world around them, flowering in all its glory, indifferent to our sorrows and yet soothing them, which brings healing and lifts the spirit. St Paul got there before Keats of course with his helpful advice in Philippians:

> Whatsoever things are lovely, whatsoever things are of good report; if there be any virtue, and if there be any praise, think on these things.

For everything we take into our minds remains there for good or ill, and to have a mind well stocked with the images and memories of beauty is to have language and resources that no isolation can remove.

But Keats goes further: he recognises that the intimations of mortality, which are also offered by the morning rose, are precisely what make its beauty so poignant and intense, that melancholy and beauty are not so far from one another, that indeed, they dwell together:

> She dwells with Beauty – Beauty that must die;
>   And Joy, whose hand is ever at his lips
> Bidding adieu …

It is no mere escapism that we should need sometimes in these sad days to revisit 'the very temple of delight', for it is given to us in this world that we should taste joy and sadness together.

75

Christmas Lights

I have not always been a fan of the ritual switching on of Christmas lights, which inevitably happens in late November, before Advent has even started. My inner liturgist was always muttering about all this premature glitz and bling, when what I felt we all needed was a slow, subfusc, understated Advent, so that we might, at least for a while, be 'the people who walked in darkness', given long enough to learn the wisdom of waiting, before, on the great day, and by glorious contrast, we would 'see his marvellous light'.

I wished in vain, of course, and I find, in any case, that I have mellowed with age. To be honest, I'm glad of any collective ritual that gathers a town or village together, affirms our life as a community, and at least gives people a chance, after the fizzy pop from various karaoke performers, to hear their own Salvation Army band play the great carols, and to get in that rare thing: a little community singing.

I had intended to go to North Walsham's big switch-on last year, but in fact it was blown away by a severe gale, which tore into the tents and booths of the hot-dog- and coffee-sellers, the charity tombola stalls, and the children's lucky dips, even before anyone had turned up. The town's health and safety officer sensed too much danger, and the whole thing was cancelled. The lights themselves came on a little later, after various repairs, but there was no one there to see them.

So, this year, I was determined to be there and make the most of it, and, in fact, I found it unexpectedly moving. Amid all the commercial bustle, the church was open, warm and welcoming, as it should be, with plenty of activities for children, and refreshments for young and old; dogs were welcome, and, indeed, I had my work cut out to keep George, our amiable greyhound, away from the mince pies and iced biscuits all temptingly displayed at nose level.

Fortified and warmed by a couple of pints from the Hop Inn, I enjoyed the gradual build-up, the growing crowd, the mothers dancing with their children on their shoulders as someone belted out 'Rockin' around the Christmas tree' from the market cross. And, while I was soaking up the atmosphere, George was hoovering up all the chips and biscuits so kindly dropped by the children.

The lights themselves, so the programme said, were to be switched on by our local MP, which is a right and proper thing for an MP of any party to do. But, just before we began our collective countdown from ten, the MP introduced his surprise guest of honour: a little boy from Ukraine, a refugee who was staying, along with his family, at the MP's house as part of the welcome and resettlement scheme.

At the end of the countdown, the boy stepped up and pressed the big red button with great glee and aplomb, and all around us the ancient market square flowered into light: trailers and streamers of little lights, looping between the shops, or hanging down from the eaves, and here and there a Bethlehem star setting out like a comet with a multi-coloured tail.

The boy who had made it all happen was enchanted, but more than one of us there were reflecting on the emblem of Advent hope which we had just witnessed, as a young refugee kindled light for us, even as his country was plunged into darkness.

76

Ear Worms

It is the time of year when I hurry through the shops, wishing I had earplugs, desperate to escape the tinny Christmas playlists that, I know, will still form little earworms in me for the rest of the day. In spite of my best endeavours, I always end up with 'Last Christmas, I gave you my heart, but the very next day you gave it away', by Wham!, playing on an endless loop, as I sit at my desk, the inane repetitions scaring off those shy poems that I was hoping to entice on to the page.

I suppose I could repurpose the song as it plays in my head, and turn it into prayer: 'This year, to save me from tears, I'll give it to someone special …' But, to be honest, giving my heart to Christ may have saved me from perdition, but it has never saved me from tears; for the thing about giving one's heart to Christ is that he keeps it supple, sensitive, full of hope, and therefore susceptible to hurt. And 'hope deferred maketh the heart sick'.

It would be easier to be cynical, easier to cheat disappointment by expecting nothing. Yet Advent – still Advent, in spite of the Christmas jingles – is all about expectation, about daring to hope again. The Latin root of 'expectation' means 'looking out', as though you looked out of a window for the long-delayed return of your beloved. George Herbert plays on that, but reverses, beautifully, the flow of the gaze; for, in his poem 'Christmas (1)', it is Christ himself who is looking out from the window of the inn, expecting Herbert:

> I took up in the next inne I could finde,
> There when I came, whom found I but my deare,
> My dearest Lord, *expecting* till the grief

Of pleasures brought me to him, readie there
To be all passengers' most sweet relief?

I'm not likely to hear Herbert's 'Christmas' on the festive playlists in Boots, although he was a dab hand at music, and a little lute music, or a madrigal, would make a nice break from Wham! and Mariah Carey.

But I still find, along with Herbert, some 'sweet relief', some companionship, in knowing that, if my hope is deferred, then so is Christ's. God knows the disappointments that I have visited on Christ, the deferral of his hopes in me which he has had to cope with till I turn and return, let alone the vulnerable hope that he places in millions of others. But he has not given up; he still keeps hoping, still expecting, looking out for us. Maybe those Wham! lyrics, still running round my head, have more to say than I thought: 'I keep my distance, but you still catch my eye, Tell me … do you recognise me?'

We have so many stratagems for keeping our distance, but, somehow, even amid the tinsel, he can still catch our eye, still give us that come-hither look. And then, however slowly, we might turn, we might move, from expectation to recognition.

Acknowledgements and References

Berry, Wendell, 'II', in *This Day: Collected and New Sabbath Poems*, Counterpoint, 2013, p. 8.

Causley, Charles, 'Eden Rock', in *Collected Poems*, Macmillan, 1992, p. 405.

Guite, Malcolm, *David's Crown*: 'LXXXIV Quam dilecta!', p. 84; 'XXIX Afferte Domino', p. 29; 'CXXXVII Super flumina', p. 137; 'Psalm 21: XXI Domine, in virtute tua', p. 21; 'Psalm 81: Exultate Deo', p. 81; Canterbury Press, 2021.

Guite, Malcolm, 'Our Burning World' is used by permission of Stainer & Bell Ltd, 23 Gruneisen Road, London N3 1LS, www.stainer.co.uk. All rights reserved.

Guite, Malcolm, *Parable and Paradox*: 'Ode to St Celia', p. 4; 'Nicholas Ferrar', p. 15; 'St Valentine', p. 12; Canterbury Press, 2016.

Guite, Malcolm, 'St Etheldreda', uncollected poem. The phrase 'nevertheless she persisted' was used by Senate Majority Leader Mitch McConnell about his attempts to silence Elizabeth Warren and has since become a feminist slogan see https://en.wikipedia.org/wiki/Nevertheless,_she_persisted.

Guite, Malcolm, 'Holding and Letting Go', in *The Singing Bowl*, Canterbury Press, 2013, p. 63.

Guite, Malcolm, *Sounding The Seasons*: 'The Ascension', p. 45; 'Baptism', p. 52; 'Candlemas', p. 25; 'Ash Wednesday', p. 26; 'The call of the disciples', p. 21; 'Trinitie Sunday', p. 48; 'Pentecost', p. 47; 'Hide and Seek', p. 50; Canterbury Press, 2012.

Guite, Malcolm, 'This Breathless Earth (John 20.19)', in *Stations of the Resurrection*, Church House Publishing, 2024.

Heaney, Seamus, 'Crediting Poetry', in *Opened Ground*, Faber & Faber, 1998, p. 458.

Heaney, Seamus, 'Bone Dreams', in *North,* Faber & Faber, 1975, p. 19.

Hughes, Ted, 'That Morning', in *Ted Hughes Collected Poems*, Paul Keegan (ed.), Faber & Faber, 2003, p. 663.

Larkin, Philip, 'To The Sea', in *High Windows*, Faber & Faber, 1974, p. 9.

Masefield, John, 1914, https://www.thespicery.com/blogs/spice-travels/stwp-1485.

Owen, Wilfred, *The War Poems of Wilfred Owen*, John Stallworthy (ed.), 1994, p. 12.

Scott, David, 'The Surplice', in *Playing For England*, Bloodaxe, 1989.

Thomas, R. S., 'The Small Window', in R. S. Thomas, *Not That He Brought Flowers*, Hart Davis, 1968.

Yeats, W. B., 'The Secret Rose' and 'The Fascination with What's Difficult', in *Collected Poems of W. B. Yeats*, Richard J. Finneran (ed.), Macmillan 1935, p. 77 and pp. 230-1.

Printed in the USA
CPSIA information can be obtained
at www.ICGtesting.com
JSHW020144201024
71960JS00007B/75